THE CREATIVE LEADER

WHAT EVERY LEADER SHOULD
KNOW ABOUT THE ART & SCIENCE
OF CREATIVE INTELLIGENCE

BOB BODEN & DR. ROB CARPENTER

DISCLAIMER:

This book is intended to inspire and guide readers toward achieving their full creative and leadership potential. However, no specific results can be promised or guaranteed. This book does not contain medical, legal, or financial advice. For such advice, please consult a qualified professional.

Book Design by: Hmdpublishing

Published by:

SoulCraft Media

Los Angeles, CA

ISBN: 979-8-9906383-4-1 (hardcover)
ISBN: 979-8-9906383-6-5 (paperback)
ISBN: 979-8-9906383-5-8 (ebook)

Publisher's Cataloging-In-Publication Data

Names:

Carpenter, Rob, 1985- author.
Boden, Bob, author.

Title:

The Creative Leader / Dr. Rob Carpenter and Bob Boden.

Description:

Los Angeles: SoulCraft Media, [2025] | Includes bibliographical references and index.

Subjects:

Leadership. | Creative ability in business. | Strategic planning. | Teams in the workplace. | Business innovation.

Classification:

LCC HD57.7 (print) | LCC HD57.7 (ebook) | DDC 658.4/092--dc23

DEDICATION

Bob Boden: To Dr. Rob, many thanks for your friendship and mentorship, and for suggesting that we partner on this exciting project. To Marla, Micki and Rachel, I love you and appreciate your support for everything I take on. To my industry and academic friends and associates, I hope that you enjoy this volume and find it valuable. Thanks for playing!

Dr. Rob Carpenter: To my family and friends, thank you for always being there for me and helping me become more than I ever thought possible. To Bob, you've been a great collaborator and friend, and I couldn't have done this without you. To my editor, Dr. Candice D. Carpenter, thank you for your insightful edits and additions to the manuscript, as you worked tirelessly to make the book accessible for lay people and other leadership gurus like yourself. And to all of the leaders reading this book: I strongly believe in you and your ability to become more creative than ever before.

CREATIVE LEADERSHIP:

*the ability to influence and guide others toward
creating new ideas, novel innovations,
and achieving original goals*

*"Innovation distinguishes
between a leader and a follower."*
— **Steve Jobs**

AUTHORS' NOTE

On a warm summer night years ago, we—Bob and Rob, as some know us—met on the Hollywood backlot of Radford Studios in Studio City; we were attending the welcome dinner for the Syracuse University Los Angeles Semester program. Our friendship was instant and electric.

Soon after, we started talking about ways we might be able to 'play' together—or work on something professionally that would be mutually satisfying, fulfilling, and meaningful. This book is a result of our play.

From the beginning, we were intent on writing about creative leadership not only because it is an often overlooked field, but also because many people consider us to be creative leaders. We were intent on writing about it because we felt we could bring a multigenerational, diverse, and unusual perspective to the topic.

Bob, for example, is a Baby Boomer, and longtime Hollywood producer and original team member of the Game Show Network who served on the Board of the Television Academy for 13 years, among many other accomplishments. Rob, on the other hand, is a Millennial and multi-hyphenate who has worked as a novelist and writer, as well as in politics, tech start-ups, and the entertainment biz.

Put differently, we wanted to write this text because we are coming from different lived experiences and vantage points. We wanted to combine our perspectives—to give you a more holistic flavor, so to speak—of what makes a creative leader. And although both of us are also professors, we wanted to make sure this book was as practical and accessible as possible. Bogging you down in unnecessary minutiae and distracting jargon was not our aim.

To help us with crafting the topics and stories for this book, some of the best and most representative producers in Hollywood agreed to share their creative wisdom so that you might be able to apply it to whatever field you find yourself in. From old school producers of *The Brady Bunch* and *Gilligan's Island*, to mid-school producers of shows like *Jeopardy!* and *Wheel of Fortune*, to new school producers of hits like *Hell's Kitchen* and *Black-ish*—and beyond—we've been blessed to curate a list of some of the most successful creative leaders from the last 60 years in show business. Collectively, they have produced thousands of television shows and movies, earned countless Oscars, Emmys®, and other awards. They've achieved blockbuster cultural and financial dreams. To these producers—including Andrew Carlberg, Jonathan Murray, Cybill Liu, Harry Friedman, Fanshen Cox, Lloyd J. Schwartz, Javier Chapa, Allison Grodner, Laura Gutin, Arthur Smith, and Stephanie Drachkovitch—we offer our sincere thanks for your time, generosity, and wonderful insights. You are dear friends, colleagues, and partners-in-crime. our contributions and experiences will help light the way for countless more people both inside and outside of Hollywood.

And to our readers, thank you too: you taking the time to read this book truly means a lot to us, especially when you could be doing other things with your day. Our goal was not only to inspire you, but also give you practical tools for becoming more creative in your own leadership journey. We believe that this creative intelligence recipe—the creative sauce that already exists within you—can be drawn out further and further to make you the best possible creative leader you can be.

TABLE OF CONTENTS

FOREWARD
BY VANCE VAN PETTEN

If you are reading this, it is reasonable to assume you are seeking inspiration and guidance for developing your creative leadership skills and abilities. This is exactly where I found myself after spending years leading the business and legal departments at three different Hollywood studios, including Paramount, Fox, and Universal. While I had worked with great leaders who operated on the corporate side of the business (the "biz" in "Showbiz"), I was uniquely inspired by the individuals leading the "show" side of it: the creative entrepreneurs who were dancing the incredibly delicate tightrope between art on the one hand and business on the other. In this world, which moved at the speed of light, new ideas and creative solutions were the keys to not only artistic success but also financial success too. And it was in this world that I saw the power of creative leadership up close and personal—ultimately drawing me in to the point I became the head of The Producers Guild of America—which allowed me to more fully realize that this type of mixed artistic and business leadership is one of the most powerful forces shaping not only Hollywood's future, but also the world's future (regardless of industry, sector, or geographic location). This book takes a deep dive into the art and science behind creative leadership and rests on the experiences of an unexpected yet highly relevant group who knows more about the topic than any other—movie and television producers, the ultimate creative leaders entrepreneurially guiding the making of the world's blockbuster films, hit shows, and formation of its culture and subcultures.

You see, producers are uniquely qualified to be creative leaders. For one, they are natural problem solvers. They operate in environments that are high-stakes, time-sensitive, and sometimes chaotic. They manage countless moving parts, unexpected disruptions, and competing interests. They know how to balance the big vision with meticulous attention to detail, all while keeping a team inspired, a project on track, and a budget intact. For them, every day brings new challenges, each one demanding quick thinking, a calm mind, and the ability to pivot on a dime. In other words, producers operate in an incredibly competitive business and organizational environment. Seamlessly, they navigate bureaucracies, logistics, investors, interest groups and the other pressures and traps of "the system."

But what makes their approach to leadership so distinctive from that of, say, traditional leadership? First, they understand the power of storytelling and its capacity to engage, persuade, and inspire not only audiences, customers, or financiers but also their own teams. They know that a clear, compelling narrative can rally a team behind-the-scenes around a shared purpose. Everyone, from directors to assistants, can be brought into alignment toward a common goal. In the boardroom, as on set, they understand that a compelling vision creatively told holds everything together.

Producers are also experts in team dynamics and talent maximization. In their world, talent is everything—but only if it can work together cohesively both in front of the camera and behind it. In other words, producers know how to persuasively bring together hundreds if not thousands of diverse personalities, perspectives, and skill sets for a singular project. They create environments where ideas can flourish and tensions can be harnessed to build stories and change our culture. These are skills that every leader needs, whether they are managing a small startup or leading a global corporation.

Finally, producers embody resilience. In an industry where setbacks are inevitable and where uncertainty is constant, they have mastered the art of bouncing back. They know how to pivot, find alternative solutions, and remain calm under pressure—qualities essential to any leader navigating today's complex, fast-paced world.

This book captures the unique insights and invaluable creative leadership lessons that ten seasoned producers bring to the table. Through stories, case studies, and practical advice, it explores what it means to lead creatively, to motivate a team with vision and empathy, and to transform challenges into opportunities. The lessons here are timeless and universal. Anyone who aspires to lead with purpose and originality can apply them in any industry.

May this book inspire you to embrace your own creative potential and unlock the artistic leader within.

Vance Van Petten

Former Executive Director, Producers Guild of America

Los Angeles, CA 2024

NOW COMING CENTER STAGE: THE CREATIVE LEADER

"Creativity is intelligence having fun."[1]
— **Albert Einstein**

The unnamed British professor, one of the most traditional of men and analytical thinkers there was, became a cult figure. He had women, men, students, and people from all kinds of backgrounds throwing themselves at him. In fact, he even cut off his phone and moved to a secret location so he couldn't be found.

Day after day, month after month, and year after year, letters would arrive describing how much of a genius he was. How he had upended people's lives. How he had ushered them into a world that the best of fantasies couldn't match.

But how did this middle age professor, known for his personal religiosity and obscure academic interests, become a cult leader?

The answer: he never started out trying to be one.

It was all a happy accident. A chance phenomenon. Luck of the draw.

Or was it?

Years earlier, this professor decided to do something his colleagues at Oxford weren't known for: become curious about his students.

He would come to class and, instead of him telling them "how it was," he playfully allowed them to tell him how it was.

The highly analytical professor became so interested in his interactions with his students that he realized that what they were saying—their expansive ideas and perspectives on the world and the colorful stories they were articulating—needed to be included in his own more narrow thinking. They needed to be included in his understanding of life to get him to see reality differently.

So he decided to do just that: integrate the ideas they jointly came up with in impromptu class sessions, and the rest, as they say, is history.

This professor, who studied obscure languages, ended up becoming one of the best selling authors of all time, precisely because he improvised, formed a creative team with his students, got their advice, and widened his view of the world. His name is, of course, J.R.R. Tolkien, the author of *The Lord of the Rings*.

And he did the things that every great creative leader does when producing something spectacularly new: marry hard-fought analytical thinking (the so-called "left side of the brain") with sweeping creativity (the so-called "right side"); deep experience (of study, of age, and of wisdom) with unexpected perspectives (of youth and vibrancy and spontaneity); a realistic mindset shaped by experience (and rules and limitations) with an idealistic one cultivated by the impossible (the idea that you might as well swing for the fences).

In other words, what Tolkien did in creating *The Lord of The Rings* are the kinds of creative leadership behaviors that Hollywood producers, half a century after he first introduced the world to his Hobbits and Snow-trolls and Fellbeasts, did when they brought his creation to the big screen for millions to see.

Put differently, these Hollywood producers, even though they weren't writers like Tolkien, engaged in the same creative process as him to technologically produce what no one thought was possible at the time. And along the way, they epitomized what it means to be a creative leader. Producers are, after all, the curious, improvisational people who take ideas and make them come to life in the face of vast uncertainty; the ones who balance a narrow understanding of strategic planning, budgets, contracts, bureaucracies, and algorithms on the one hand, with bubbling artistic talent and innovation on the other. They are the types of leaders that the world needs most right now in every industry across the globe—the ones with the creative intelligence that will be the meta leadership skill of the future.

After decades of excellent books about leadership featuring the voices of traditional corporate CEOs, military strategists, and political officials—and leadership books featuring the voices of creative tech titans—we felt it was time to feature a unique group of leaders who, as a professional group or class, best combine the analytical and creative in their day-to-day jobs. By focusing on media leaders, we wanted to give you a roadmap for your own creative leadership journey. Why? Because media producers have often been ignored, overlooked, and dismissed in these types of leadership books. They have been palpably absent not only from an artistic or cultural appreciation point of view, but also from a leadership and management one.

The thinking and skills needed to successfully navigate the world of uncertainty, rapid technological upheaval, innovative competitors, and rapidly changing consumer preferences that we find ourselves in are what every leader (inside and) outside Hollywood needs to learn. And these producers can teach us how to learn them.

Though this book focuses on the ideas and stories of producers in film and television, it is for any leader in any sector, especially for the leaders who realize that relying on the old ways of doing things are not working from a financial and human performance point of view. These old ways include the following:

- *fear*
- *top down and transactional communication and interactions*
- *resistance to change and risk aversion*
- *a short-term focus*
- *lack of transparency*
- *overemphasis on individual achievement*
- *hierarchy*
- *one-size-fits-all management*
- *ignoring mental health and emotional intelligence*
- *single-career paths*
- *solo decision making*
- *disregarding feedback from junior employees*
- *lack of interdisciplinary approaches, and*
- *conformity over creativity*

This book is for the leaders who realize that relying on traditional leadership approaches has caused 150% less market share and 350% less revenue growth for companies [2]

And it's for the leaders who realize that the human toll traditional leadership has taken is even worse than its financial one—with the majority of workers feeling disengaged from their jobs; working people running on burnout; and the average professional questioning whether their job is even worth it.

In other words, this book is for the leaders who are starting to see that traditional leadership does not work—and should be buried in the graveyard. Interestingly, more and more employees are starting to see this too. According to Harvard Business Review, for example, more than 70% of employees state that their organization's leaders DO NOT know how to foster creativity, innovative solutions, or produce real change at their workplaces so that they can fix all that ails them.[3]

This is why we wrote this book: to help you overcome the trap of traditional leadership bias that has been foisted upon you. We encourage you to enlarge your lens of focus and become the creative leader your organization needs you to be—and so that you can become the creative leader *the world needs you to be.*

We believe that by learning to creatively see the world from the unending combinations of hues and colors—like the brightest kaleidoscope you could ever imagine— you can do this. And we believe the benefits for you, for your organization, and for society will be enormous. After reading this book, you will acquire the following benefits:

- Gaining new insights about the recipe for creative intelligence: namely, the role curiosity, optimism, play, storytelling, divergent hiring, competing with emotion, decision strategy, crisis management, weak-tie mentorship, and improvisational intelligence factor into your day-to-day leadership;

- Boosting your mental, emotional, and workplace well-being through practices that creatively lead to increased levels of dopamine (the pleasure chemical), serotonin (the relaxation chemical), and oxytocin (the trust and bonding chemical);

- Being equipped with specific creative leadership strategies, practices, exercises, and approaches so you can hit the ground running today—not some time in the distant future.

Of course, the benefits do not start and end there, but we just wanted to give you a quick preview of what you will be receiving by taking this short journey toward more creative leadership in your own life and career.

To help us out with this, we have extensively interviewed multiple Oscar®, Grammy®, Emmy®, and Peabody®-winning Hollywood producers. They have invited us into their world and shared their creative leadership process, and the strategies they use to achieve individual and organizational peak performance. They have shown us how to truly balance analytical thinking and algorithmic data on the one hand, with creativity and imagination on the other. It is our hope that you find both inspiration in their stories and practical ideas and strategies you can use in your own life right away. So without further ado, let's get started on your journey to creative leadership.

CHAPTER 1

CREATIVE INTELLIGENCE IS A SKILL TO BE LEARNED, NOT AN IMMUTABLE TRAIT BESTOWED AT BIRTH

"You can't use up creativity. The more you use, the more you have."[1]
— **Maya Angelou**

For decades, Jonathan Murray, the Mississippi-born Hollywood hopeful, saw that the entertainment industry was only interested in producing one kind of show: scripted television.

This can't be the only way, he thought to himself. Surely entertainment can go beyond half hour sit-coms and hour dramas? Surely real life, if properly shot and edited, can be as or more compelling than any scripted show?

But the television studios and networks didn't see it that way. Their traditional business model worked, they assured themselves, and they were sure that the wild ideas of Jonathan Murray and his business partner, the late Mary Ellis Bunim, would not. In fact, according to studies from Harvard Business Review and the Gallup Organization, these TV execs fell into the trap that up to 70% of all organizations do across almost every industry: being fearful of, and resistant to, change and new ideas.[2]

But Mary-Ellis and Jonathan kept pushing against the industry's institutional conservatism. They knew that the rigid entertainment hierarchies and the well-documented status-quo bias could be overcome if only somebody would take a chance on them and their concepts.

So, they pitched Murray's show to the only place that would give him a chance: an upstart television Network which saw potential. You see, Mary-Ellis and Jonathan wanted to film real people from different backgrounds and put them in a house together. They wanted to do away with scripts and see what type of soap-opera drama would unfold. They argued that this model would not only be cheaper to shoot, but also faster to produce; it could generate more revenue than anyone in Hollywood realized.

The Network liked what they heard but they still didn't want to really risk it. So they compromised on his idea and decided to film real people with a script.

And guess what? They failed dramatically.

The project was just too unwieldy. But instead of pulling the plug completely, they decided to give Jonathan's idea a second chance by using his original concept instead. This time it worked. *The Real World* was thus born on MTV in 1992 and revolutionized television, perhaps forever, by ushering in unscripted narrative TV as a brand new genre.[3]

And while Jonathan and Mary-Ellis were busy filming—too busy to even celebrate the success of their own creation—the entire Hollywood ecosystem was studying what they were doing. And in time, they started to realize that, instead of trying to conserve the familiar past like they had been doing, maybe they should be bold and push toward a more creative future. Of course, it didn't hurt that Bunim and Murray proved their innovation substantially helped Tinseltown in the ratings and revenue business, but we digress.

As important as anything else, Hollywood was starting to learn not just about what Jonathan and Mary-Ellis were doing as they closely studied the particulars of their show. They were starting to learn something about creative leadership too that seemed to have escaped them for a time: *creative leadership is about influencing and guiding others toward <u>creating new ideas</u>, <u>novel innovations</u>, and <u>achieving original goals</u>, not just defaulting to old and predictable ones (the goals of traditional leadership).*

In other words, what Hollywood discovered was the huge distinction between traditional leadership on the one hand and creative leadership on the other. For example:

Traditional Leadership vs.	**Creative Leadership**
Prizes old and predictable goals and outcomes	Craves original and innovative ideas and results
Relies on established problem solving techniques	Uses unconventional and frequently non-linear problem solving
Resistant to most risk and change	Cautiously optimistic about introducing change
Top-down control	Collaboration mixing bottom up, top-down, and sideways-out influence
Formal, authoritative communication styles	Informal, colloquial style of communication
Focuses on efficiency and productivity	Focuses on experimentation
Prioritizes analysis on singular firm/industry	Prioritizes intuition and mixing proven ideas and solutions from multiple industries
Uncomfortable with uncertainty	Thrives on ambiguity
Fixed and rigid	Flexible and nimble
Adheres to established norms and practices	Pushes boundaries
Limited openness to feedback	Substantial openness to feedback
Competition and short-term results are core values	Curiosity and long-term change are core values
One "right" way to do things	Many "right" ways to do things
The Past	The Future

Jonathan told us, after thinking about one of the main take-aways of creative leadership himself:

> *"I think in my early days of being a leader, I didn't realize that there were multiple ways to lead because I think most of the leaders that I saw were these take no prisoners super macho type people [traditional leaders]. As I saw other people lead, I realized that there's more than one way to be successful."*

Put differently, Jonathan realized there is more than one way to lead—and how liberating this was as a creative leader. It was liberating because it was so antithetical to everything he not only personally observed, but was taught growing up.

For example, from grade school onward society teaches everyone, leaders included, that there is only "one right answer." And while this might be true for mathematics or empirical science, it is not true in leadership (or in countless other endeavors of life). In his seminal book *Multiple Intelligences*, Harvard's Howard Gardner shows us that there are in fact eight major types of intelligences—linguistic and mathematical intelligences, intrapersonal and musical intelligences, and a few others—but the one that our country most emphasizes is logical or analytical intelligence.[4] The one that says "there is only one answer, one path, one direction, and if you don't go down it, you're wrong." This is why the SAT, for example, only tests cognitive abilities like reading and math, but not artistic ones, people skills, emotional intelligence, athletic talent, or all of the other intelligences that can and do make people successful in life. The SAT doesn't test them because there is no "one right answer" for these subjects, and therefore they exclude these diverse intelligences altogether, leaving millions of students feeling unseen, unheard, and underappreciated Without the ability to objectively prove they have diverse and valuable skills, students are limited in their ability to showcase skills important to their long-term growth, potential, and success. Not only is this short sighted by testing agencies, but also contradicted by research from the Nobel Prize-winning economist James Heckman which acknowledges that traditional SAT-tested IQ only accounts for about 2% of people's career success.[5]

But many traditional leaders embrace the exclusion of most intelligence types by overly relying on analytical intelligence, which is the one right answer approach to problem-solving, people management, and leadership. It is a type of thinking that never stops to think there might be other (and better) ways to lead. These leaders have let the "one right answer" SAT ideology define their leadership in practice. Not only do they see nothing wrong with this, but they also have never even admitted this as a problem in the first place. This is how blinded to multiple intelligences, including creative intelligence, many of them seem to be. If not in talk, but definitely in action. Recall that 70% of employees do not believe their leaders or workplaces are creative or know how to introduce creative change initiatives to fix the many ills of their organizations. So despite the talk of many traditional leaders saying they desire creativity in their workplace, they don't seem to be backing it up with their actual practices and behaviors. Deep down, they implicitly assume there is only one right way that just so happens to be synonymous with their preferred way, as opposed to one of many ways things could creatively get done.

But this focusing on clinging to the one right answer, this overemphasis on cognitive intelligence at the expense of other types of intelligences, is wrong. All the new scientific literature on leadership and success proves it wrong, as does our own life experience (and perhaps yours too). As Bob said at one of our lunches when we were putting together this book, "I've given up my need to be right" and instead focus on what's needed— and the most optimal path forward.

For Jonathan, realizing that success was not a singular or monolithic concept, but a dynamic one, was empowering. By understanding that leadership is less about finding the one right way, but instead about being adaptable and exploring multiple possible right ways, he was personally learning the principles that guide excellence in creative leadership. By no longer chaining himself to narrow minded and outdated approaches like the conventional wisdom of the past or stultifying metrics of the present, he allowed his curiosity to be unleashed for greater and greater returns. Thus, as a creative leader, he has never looked back.

But we know what you might be thinking. And we've heard it a thousand times: "it's great that other people like Jonathan are creative leaders, but I'm not that creative"...or "I don't know how to be creative and would get stuck or embarrass myself if I tried." Or some version of this that many amazing people in society have convinced themselves of to justify why they do not want to invest in their own creative intelligence. But the reality is you <u>can</u> teach an old dog new tricks, including creative leadership ones. It just so happens that neuroscience, or brain science, proves it.

For example, the human brain has a remarkable ability to change. Despite myths to the contrary, it doesn't stop growing or changing at 26 years old). So at almost any age in life, you can deliberately create new neural pathways in your brain because of the brain's inherent neuroplasticity, or ability to change. Thus, you can strengthen a divergent skill like creativity—and listless other skills—throughout your entire life .[6] Without oversimplifying things too much, the basal ganglia region of the brain can predominantly assist with new learning and habit-building creative behaviors, little by little, throughout your lifetime.[7]

In other words, our ability to change and be creative is based on our motivation and commitment to building better brains.

Not some innate or elusive "creativity gene" we feel we were never born with, or believe we can never learn how to use, is the cause. Let's let this sink in: to become more creative, or more creatively intelligent, we have to think of it as a muscle we are building—not just some immutable trait we possess at birth or lose in childhood. Because creative intelligence is a skill to be developed, and not a trait that is passed on like genetics, it is surprisingly very learnable, practicable, and doable at any point in a person's life. And it is a skill that every type of leader should be working hard to develop.

For example:

- **Visionary Leaders** focus on inspiration and long-term goals. They can propose out of the box and creative solutions for reaching these goals;

- **Democratic Leaders** encourage participation and can leverage creativity during collaborative brainstorming sessions;

- **Autocratic & Transactional Leaders** issue directives and can employ a variety of creative ways to reach them;

- **Transformational Leaders** are empowering and can utilize creativity to help drive the bold change and innovation they seek;

- **Servant Leaders** focus on the needs of others; they can be more effective in doing this by equipping themselves with creative ideas, strategies, and approaches;

- **Charismatic Leaders** use their enthusiasm and persuasion skills to inspire action. They can best do this implementing relying on a creative vision; and

- **Laissez-Faire Leaders** are hands-off, which can counterintuitively allow creative ideas and autonomy to flourish in the hands of the right team members.

Regardless of whatever leadership philosophy you ascribe to and practice—whether it be a visionary, democratic, autocratic, transformational, servant, charismatic, or laissez-faire leadership style—the creative leadership skill is compatible with any and all of these. There is no need to fear making a substantial investment in creative leadership at the expense of other types of leadership.

So it is clear: by becoming more of a creative leader, you can still make it mesh with your current leadership style. By the way, if you want to know the truth about the different leadership approaches above, all of the empirical data shows that Transformational Leaders are typically the most effective leaders, and that Autocratic and Transactional Leaders are the least effective leaders. Depending on the context, Democratic, Charismatic, Servant, and Laissez-Faire leaders can be useful.).[8] Of course, many leaders use a situational approach, or a mixture of the above approaches. Nonetheless, creative leadership is still compatible with whatever path one takes. This is why anecdotes abound about leaders who are extremely creative but who are all over the map when it comes to their overall leadership philosophy.

As Jonathan has taught us, creative intelligence is really just the practiced skill of recognizing that there are lots of different and original ways to look at something—and multiple original paths toward reaching a goal. The SAT model of leadership, the one right answer approach that is used for problem solving, people management,and the like, is really just creative incompetence that has not been exposed as such until now. It is disguised as "logic" and "managing a status quo". It refuses to see the truth of a multi-colored world because it has convinced everyone that the world only exists in black and white (or perhaps shades of gray, which is just as underwhelming and unworkable in a rapidly changing world).

CASE STUDY: BREAKING THE MOLD: JONATHAN MURRAY'S UNSCRIPTED REVOLUTION

Jonathan Murray disrupted Hollywood in the same way as Netflix disrupted Blockbuster, Airbnb disrupted hotels, and Amazon disrupted retail. His idea of filming real people in real-life circumstances without a script was, quite frankly, radical. Today, of course, it is a given that reality television is a common form of entertainment but this is in large part thanks to Jonathan's persistence and ingenuity to make it one of the preferred forms of consumption. With the groundbreaking success *of The Real World*, he proved that unscripted narrative TV could captivate audiences and generate significant revenue, upending nearly 100 years of narrow-thinking and corporate dogma about what success "looked like" in Tinseltown. Without exaggerating too much, what Jonathan did as a creative leader was change not only what Hollywood did, but also how Hollywood did it, and not only what they thought, but how they thought about it.

Just as important, what he did was show Hollywood the personal distinctions between the traditional leaders many of them had become and the creative leader he was . For example, Jonathan showed them that they were prizing old and predictable goals, over-relying on established problem-solving techniques, and resisting change, which is why they weren't seeing breakthroughs like his show.

Interestingly, Jonathan shared with us that most traditional leaders (even those in Hollywood) will not admit to others—and perhaps will not admit to themselves—that they are traditional. Instead, they demonstrate through their actions and decisions, not through their words or self-appraisals, that they prefer the status quo. In other words, they default to the "language of creativity" because it sounds good, but in practice they frequently cling to the same old ideas, policies, and approaches they've always used. They say they want creative people on their team. Yet, when they hire creatives, they refuse to consider their creative ideas, or too easily let creative ideas fizzle out and die.

Jonathan shared one way he consistently practiced creative leadership that would incorporate the creativity of his entire team, an approach that can be used by any leader in any field: "My management approach is called the Walking Around style. I would always walk over to someone's cubicle office rather than phone them or email them. There are times I would email a follow-up saying, "This is what we talked about; this is what we agreed.' But I love the idea of just walking around and popping into someone's office to talk about a situation." This hands-on, face-to-face approach illustrates his belief in the power of informal interaction that constantly generates new ideas and human warmth, a stark contrast to the impersonal and formal nature of traditional leadership communication that generates anything but novel concepts and strong interpersonal connections.

By constantly walking around and talking to his team—not just during scheduled meetings or via email or online messaging tools—Jonathan demonstrated that leadership was not just about telling people to follow the one right way he dictated to them. Instead, he showed them that it was about being adaptable and exploring numerous possible right ways, allowing curiosity, spontaneity, and experimentation to flourish—the exact prerequisites for creative possibilities to occur.

Of course, there are many other ways Jonathan's creative intelligence impacted his leadership beyond this highly interactive approach. But the main takeaway here is that, unlike traditional leaders, Jonathan was not a distant figure dictating commands from on high. He was not unwilling to break from short-term thinking, predictable goals and formulas, and limited openness to feedback. He was refreshingly just the opposite, as all creative leaders should be, by personally modeling an open mindedness and desire to make sure all people and ideas are seen, heard, understood. Demonstrating the essence of creative leadership, he scanned every possible nook and cranny for the best and most original ideas until they were found, implemented, and succeeded.

Key Takeaways

1. **Challenge Conventional Thinking:** Jonathan Murray's journey with *The Real World* shows the power of questioning established norms in entertainment. Traditional leaders often stick to proven methods, but creative leaders like Jonathan push boundaries by exploring unorthodox approaches.

2. **Embrace Adaptability:** Creative leadership involves adaptability and openness to change. Murray's persistence in refining his show despite initial setbacks underscores the importance of flexibility in leadership styles and approaches.

3. **Reject The Dangerous and Outdated Idea That There is Only One Right Way:** By understanding that there are multiple potential paths and multiple potential answers - not just one - leaders can maximize their creativity and embrace the reality of a world of many colors, not just a world of blacks and whites and possibly shades of gray.

CHAPTER 2
CURIOSITY UNLEASHED

"Curiosity is the lust of the mind."[1]
—Thomas Hobbes

What do the vast majority of Nobel Prize winners—in peace, economics, medicine, chemistry, and literature—not only have in common with each other, but also with the greatest Hollywood producers? Simply put: curiosity about, and commitment to, a creative intelligence not just within their chosen profession but also outside of it that allows them to achieve major breakthroughs.

For example, Albert Einstein, who won a Nobel Prize for discovering the photoelectric effect, was insanely curious about many things outside of science: he played the violin with chamber orchestras, wrote essays on religion and politics, and even co-founded a university (Hebrew University).[2]

Marie Curie, the first person to win a Nobel Prize in two different fields (physics and chemistry) was incredibly curious about how she could best help people–she had "interpersonal intelligence" (or "people intelligence") as Dr. Howard Gardner would say–so she devoted much of her time to humanitarian work by helping to develop the mobile X-Ray units that aided wounded soldiers in World War I and co-founded the International Red Cross.[3]

Richard Feynman, who won a Nobel Prize in physics, played music throughout his life (the bongos), and was an amateur artist who created abstract and colorful paintings because he was curious about several different things outside of science during his time on the earth.[4]

Martin Luther King Jr., who won a Nobel Prize in Peace for leading the Civil Rights Movement, regularly played the piano and was curious how he could continue improving his craft.[5] His wife Corretta was the same way: as a classically trained pianist and singer who often performed alongside Aretha Franklin, Stevie Wonder, and Nina Simone to raise funds for the Movement, she operated in multiple political, religious, and creative arenas simultaneously.[6]

Likewise, as documented in *The Polymath: Unlocking the Power of Human Versatility* by Waqas Ahmed and other great books about Renaissance Men and Women, most Nobel Prize winners have demonstrated ever-increasing curiosity about a wide variety of topics as they continue to grow, develop, and become more successful.[7] Whether it be art, music, humanitarianism, or a host of other disciplines—including, interestingly, religion and spirituality, which 90% of them explore with great enthusiasm and eventually become committed to—these winners invest in their polymathic curiosity and creativity throughout the course of their careers, just like many Hollywood producers.[8]

To make the idea of curiosity more concrete in the Hollywood context, let's think about it with some specific movies you may have seen. And let's think about it from the perspective of the creators behind these movies who refused to rest on their laurels and do the same thing twice. Steven Spielberg's *Jurassic Park* and George Lucas's *Star Wars*, for instance, are both examples of producer-directors being curious about how they could tell new stories in new ways with never before seen technologies acquired outside of the entertainment industry and even outside of Silicon Valley. Even though they had already made previous movies that were boundary-breaking, and which they could have comfortably used the same technologies for for future films, they chose to employ something fresh. In each case, they were curious about bringing in new ideas and approaches they had recently learned about from computer science to create stunning new breakthroughs (a huge novelty at the time, particularly for people in an industry that had not changed its core filming technologies in nearly a century).

Put differently, those who are considered to be the most curious people in society, like these movie creators (and our producers featured in this book), continue to invest in their own curiosity and explore new directions in sometimes unusual places despite their past successes (and sometimes failures).

What's interesting about this type of boundary-pushing curiosity is that, like creative intelligence, it too can be nurtured. One of the reasons many people find it difficult to develop, however, is the intense focus on specialization and linear thinking that society currently prizes—the so-called "SAT Ideology" we mentioned in the last chapter. Not only do universities emphasize this type of educational and career specialization that celebrates "the one right way," but so do most organizations and leaders. And the overall impacts have not always been positive.

For instance, specialization can be helpful in a predictable world: in the world of the mid to late 20th Century where rapid change, technological upheavals, and professional disruption were not common. However, hyper-specialization in our new, dramatically uncertain world can be downright counterproductive—and the one "right" way can lead down the wrong path. Focusing too much on specialization in this changing world often accomplishes the following:

- A significant lack of curiosity about the world in general, and about the "big picture" of many different fields in particular. Specialists frequently go down rabbit holes that are not useful. For example, up to 70% of all academic studies, including in both the sciences and social sciences, cannot be replicated. Perhaps this is because the "right" way many studies are designed produce specific results under specific conditions; they cannot be repeated with "different" designs under different conditions. Worse yet, they cannot be integrated into the larger whole to produce the kinds of real insights and breakthroughs we need to advance humanity forward.[9] All the while, this leads to billions of dollars spent every year on a disproportionate amount of research that is essentially not useful at best, or wasteful at worst.

- Negative impacts on mental and physical health of its specialist practitioners to a greater degree than those who do not overspecialize. The result? Stultifying black and white thinking, as mentioned in our intro, and not the kaleidoscope of colors that makes life interesting. With such an increasingly narrowed focus, individuals can act as pre-programmed "robots" or "computers" who only understand the limited algorithms they were trained to respond to. They easily become psychologically and emotionally overwhelmed and stressed – or even contemptuous and dismissive – when anything new or different gets thrown at them. This ultimately damages their physiological responses and structures in the process.[10] However, with a wider breadth of focus, their mental, emotional, and physical health can be more optimal because people experience life more as humans.

- Unnecessary communication barriers between different fields—fields which, more and more, will need to be inter-disciplinary to solve individual, organizational, and societal problems. This leads to a focus on overly technical jargon, causing people to be unable to communicate with one another, and often leading to major problems.[11] If you've ever had a health issue, for example, getting passed on from one specialist to the next, taking duplicate tests because the healthcare practitioners are not communicating with each other, experiencing changes in diagnosis because of disagreement between the healthcare practitioners, receiving overly complicated or delayed treatment, you understand first hand the type of physical, mental, and emotional harm this can cause. When specialists only know what they're doing, but don't know what everybody is doing, real issues emerge.

- Individuals who hyper-specialize are at greater career risk as new technologies quickly make their narrow skills obsolete. Speak to any travel agent, manufacturing worker, retail salesperson, paralegal, or insurance underwriter, and they will tell you the dangers first hand of skills becoming obsolete.[12] Of course, more and more specialists beyond these fields, including in medicine and many white collar professions, will be facing this threat with greater and greater urgency.

- Limited breakthrough innovations and problem solving that society needs according to David Epstein's hit book *Range: Why Generalists Triumph in a Specialized World*.[13] For example, in terms of patents issued in the last 40 years, he mentions that specialists received the majority of patents in the year 1985 but they have since fallen off of the cliff for this group, as generalists now receive the lion's share. This is likely because they have the ability to think more creatively and more curiously than the narrowly-trained hyper-specialists who are frequently blinded to many "obvious" realities the non-specialists easily see.

Of course, we are not saying that specialists do not contribute valuable things to society. We need specialized surgeons to repair malfunctioning or corrupted organs of the body, civil engineers to construct safe infrastructure, agricultural specialists to produce edible food, and so on. We are also not saying that specialists cannot be good leaders in general or even excel as leaders in certain fields, such as biotechnology, aerospace engineering, and cybersecurity, among others. They certainly can and do excel, and data suggests this is the case, especially for specialists who worked in more linear eras prior to accelerated change or market disruptions. On the other hand, it is also true according to studies that non-specialists who serve as leaders have excelled too, especially in industries like tech startups, consulting, entrepreneurship, and academic administration.

What we are saying, however, is that, when the "SAT Ideology" dictates that *most* people become specialists (over hyper-specialists, really) to pursue "the one right way," we are unnecessarily putting individuals and organizations at great risk in a variety of ways. For leaders, having a team of hyper-specialists with the same skill sets, thought processes, and professional interests—and the same blind spots because they have been trained in the same way and have the same experiences and are looking for the same "one right answer"—this is dangerous. Not only will their specializations put them at a disadvantage compared to leaders who are non-specialists—who are more adaptable, cross-disciplinary, and better able to manage change than they are—but also contribute to missed opportunities or near-missed opportunities. This happens even in the field of entertainment, where specialists sometimes cannot see beyond what they "know" or have been "trained to know".

Producer Stephanie Drachkovitch saw first hand how if she had not trained herself to be curious and look for change—something many hyper specialists "know" is impossible—a great opportunity would have passed her by.

For example, Stephanie told us that one day she was at home watching a late night talk show. And on came Mark Wahlberg who mentioned he had a brother who was chef and opening a new restaurant called "Wahlburgers." So Stephanie thought, *hmm I never knew that one of the Wahlbergs was a chef, and by naming the restaurant Wahlburgers, they obviously have a sense of humor about themselves—what if we did a family docuseries with Mark and his brother about this restaurant? Could be interesting.*

Despite Mark never having done a reality show before—something hyperspecialists in the industry (the so-called "television experts") screamed A-list celebrities would be dead set against—Stephanie felt it was at least worth the shot to see if he would. So she decided to call his agent who, very fortunately, was curious just like her and who said he would go find out to see what Mark and his family thought. Well, find out he did: they were curious about the idea and, after several meetings with Stephanie's team, said "Let's give it a go." Two Emmy® nominations and 10 seasons of The Wahlbergers later had proved her right and the hyperspecialists wrong.

This is just one example of how allowing curiosity to guide you—instead of the "this has never been done before" or "this is not the right way" or "they'll probably say 'No'" mindset that specialists usually carry because of their training or experience. And the lesson is this: you can surprise yourself—and perhaps even get some big victories along the way like Stephanie. But at the very least, when you are curious about trying new things, you will become increasingly more creative over time and receive a host of other benefits too. You will sharpen your problem-solving skills, cognitive abilities, emotional state and emotional intelligence, and strengthen your professional relationships because of the personal and professional growth you're experiencing—technically, as your brain's neuroplasticity changes, you will create new thinking patterns, skill sets, and opportunities that will improve every part of your leadership.

And even if you have significant restrictions put on you because of time, money, or other factors, you can still allow your curiosity to flourish. Lloyd J. Schwartz, a writer-producer who was part of the first "father-son" Hollywood producing team in history alongside his dad Sherwood Schwartz (creator of Gilligan's Island and The Brady Bunch), told us that constraints are actually your friend in creative leadership. For example, he said,

"I always say art is defined by its limitations. And that is a good thing for me when they tell you the size of the canvas, the size of the budget, the kind of people you have to put in it, all those things, that creates the art form for me."

It also creates the product or service innovation opportunity for any type of creative leader regardless of their chosen field of practice.

If you want to take a deeper dive into the role curiosity and constraints play in the entertainment field, check out books by Hollywood insiders like the Founder of Pixar's *Creativity Inc.* and Oscar®-winning *Apollo 13* producer Brian Grazer's *A Curious Mind* which are fascinating reads.[14][15] And if you want an even deeper dive outside of entertainment (but from a science of curiosity perspective), creativity researcher John Baer goes into depth about how you can raise your curiosity too.[16] One of the things Baer discusses is that there are two types of creativity: a general creativity (somebody who has a creative skill set applicable across multiple fields) *and* domain or industry-specific creativity (or somebody with an entirely different creativity skill set applicable to being creative in specific fields like art, technology, medicine, etc., which is the more common type of creativity and easier to access).

But for our purposes, here are three concrete ways to cultivate more curiosity in your life and creative leadership in a more general way:

1. Ask better and more penetrating questions. For example, by channeling your inner-Socrates and taking a more disciplined approach to asking questions, you can start to challenge old assumptions you have and encourage exploration. Researchers Arnaund Chevallier, Frederic Dalsace, and Jean-Louis Barsoux have provided a great framework for this. You can ask:

- **Investigative questions**: Curiously asking *why* and *how* questions about what's known about a problem or situation helps you excavate non-obvious information. For example, an investigative question could be, "Why have I not considered myself a creative person when I have the tools to increase my own creativity and curiosity according to science?"

- **Speculative questions**: Using phrases like "What if?" "What else?" "How might we?"overcomes anchoring biases, limited thinking, wrong or misleading assumptions, and helps to re-frame a situation. Asking, "What if I was more creative today than I was yesterday, and what if I am more creative tomorrow than I am today? How will my career and leadership look different?"

- **Productive questions**: Asking "Now what?" questions help to determine your capacity for dealing with a situation, what resources you invest in it, and other risks. For instance, by asking yourself, "Now what do I specifically do to increase my creativity bit by bit?", you can cultivate more curiosity.

- **Interpretative questions**: "So what?" inquiries like "What did we learn from this?" or "How is this useful?" or "Are we asking the right questions?" helps draw out eventual consequences or implications of your thinking and approach. In your own life, asking "So what is the point of all of this curiosity? To create more solutions? To relate better to people? To make better decisions? To be a more effective leader?" are helpful.

Jonathan Murray, whom you met in the last chapter, told us about a time he helped an editor for one of his many shows be more curious and ask questions just like the above. He said:

"There were so many times I had to say to the editor: 'Well, look, if you don't think what I'm saying is right, I need you to question me on it. Don't just take my note and do it without ever being curious about it or asking why I gave the note or asking me different questions, so we can make things better.' The reason the show is great is because the material is tested at every level in the process and everyone is empowered to make the show better by asking tough, curious, creative questions."

2. **You can also hone your curiosity by diversifying the types of books you read, videos you watch, people you listen to, and experiences you engage in.** There are collectively millions of qualified voices outside of your industry who exist in the world; for example, who could help you see the world differently than you do right now. Many of them have documented their learning which is easily accessible. Firms like Silicon Valley-based IDEO and the late Steve Jobs both attribute to their success "borrowing" ideas outside of their core field of expertise or industry and applying them, making them perceived geniuses in the process. In fact, most of Jobs's major "creative innovations," from the mouse to the iPod to iTunes to touchscreens on the iPhone to tablets and Apple's store designs, were "borrowed" from things he saw other people doing in other industries.

To put some icing on this point, Stephanie said,

"Whenever we're interviewing possible team members, I want to know what you read and what you watch…What do you consume? How do you get your news? What do you read outside of industry stuff? I mean, industry stuff is important, absolutely, but what else do you read and watch?"

Three practical but creative ways to implement diversifying your information consumption and learning could be: using **Multimodal-Learning** or learning things through multiple senses—reading, writing, listening, and playing—to understand them more comprehensively than just trying to understand using only one sense.[18] For instance, to improve your curiosity you could simultaneously read books and articles about it, listen to podcasts, write an article about what you're learning, and playfully test a hypothesis about curiosity in the real world (i.e., like how your sensory experiences change when exposed to a new cuisine or music you don't listen to and how it impacts your curiosity). This will stimulate activity in different parts of your brain and cause you to accelerate your understanding of the topic, change your neural networks, and experience the topic in different ways;

Brute-Force learning: learning one topic from multiple sources or voices at once, like learning about curiosity strategies by reading, watching, or listening to the works of curiosity experts like Todd Kashen, Susan Engel, and Mario Livio at the same time to get a richer and more saturated perspective on the topic[19];

And **Pyramid Learning**: rehearsing learning continuously as you absorb new information by starting at the bottom of a pyramid with 6. first grasping the concept; 5. moving to the next level to recall it; 4. Explaining it in your own words; 3. Applying your learning practically; 2. Analyzing the results once you've applied them; and 1. Creating your own personalized model of understanding.[20]

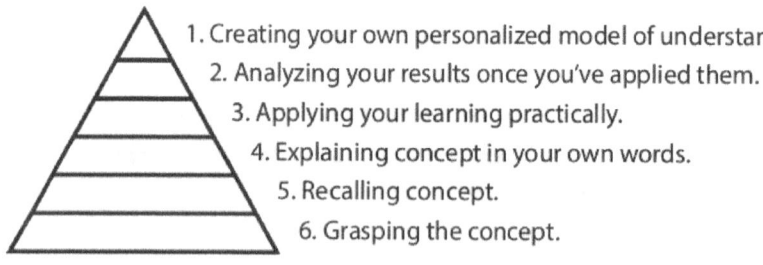

1. Creating your own personalized model of understanding.
2. Analyzing your results once you've applied them.
3. Applying your learning practically.
4. Explaining concept in your own words.
5. Recalling concept.
6. Grasping the concept.

3. **Embrace a "learn well" instead of "do well" attitude.** The most creative and curious leaders see that this is not a word game; there is a substantial performance difference in

seeing yourself as somebody who learns well compared to somebody who performs well. In her phenomenal book *Insight*, for example, Dr. Tasha Eurich cites the fact that people who primarily see themselves as individuals who learn well are more adaptable, innovative, skill-oriented, resilient, productive, successful and professionally satisfied than those who are focused on "doing well.[21] The latter is a fixed-mindset, while the former is a growth mindset and is the approach that most of the world's peak performers take, whether they be Olympians, astronauts, professional athletes, Nobel Prize winners, or yes, Hollywood producers. Their curiosity about learning, in other words, is a major part of what fuels their elite performance and causes them to "do well."

It is clear from all of this that there are well-honed strategies to increase your curiosity so that you can become a more creative leader. Not only will you push back against the "one right way" attitude that stifles much contemporary leadership and progress, you will over time become more flexible and better able to learn different ways to get things done. Of course, for micromanagers and control freak style leaders this is bad news because they want things done their way. They consciously or subconsciously (and wrongly) believe their way is the only way and synonymous with the right way. Yet, these types of leaders are dramatically less effective, according to empirical evidence, than they are assumed to be.[22] Not only do they decrease employee morale and satisfaction, hinder productivity, reduce financial earnings, and increase their team's stress and burnout, but they often end up harming themselves in the process.[23] That is why they, and all of us, should invest in curiosity to get more things done in a less stressful, more productive, and more creative way.

CASE STUDY: CURIOSITY UNBOUND: THE BOLD LEADERSHIP OF STEPHANIE DRACHKOVITCH

Stephanie Drachkovitch is known for her relentless pursuit of new knowledge and curiosity, both for the sake of learning new things but also for the practical desire to always bring unique ideas to the table. "Curiosity keeps me engaged and excited about what we do," she told us. "It drives me to ask questions, seek out new stories, and push boundaries."

Stephanie's curiosity has been instrumental in the success of 44 Blue Productions, a production company she co-founded with her husband Rasha that is renowned for its innovative and diverse content across numerous networks and streaming platforms. In shows ranging from *Wahlburgers* to *Lockup*, NBC's *LA Fire & Rescue*, A&E's *Nightwatch*, E!'s *Hollywood Medium with Tyler Henry*, Netflix's *Life After Death With Tyler Henry*, and Animal Planet's *Pit Bulls & Parolees* and beyond, she has encouraged her team to think outside the box and embrace unconventional approaches. This has led to the discovery and exposure of stories that have shocked, informed and fascinated millions of people throughout the world. "In our industry, things are constantly changing... curiosity helps us stay ahead of the curve by continuously learning and making sure we are always trying to figure new things out."

Stephanie's approach to curiosity in general and creative leadership in particular is deeply rooted in her belief in the importance of asking lots of questions she does not know the answer to, something many traditional leaders are afraid to do. "I find that repeating back to someone what they've said, to make sure I understand an assignment or an expectation, is really helpful. I want to make sure that I'm not afraid to ask to clarify things for a client or a 'superior' or somebody we're working for. I think sometimes people get shy about that, like we don't want to look like we don't know or we don't want to look stupid, so we're afraid to ask. But you know a long time ago someone taught me that the only stupid question is the one that is not asked. So I've gained a lot of confidence over the years about not being afraid to ask that question, sometimes without finding the right time to ask it."

This willingness to ask questions, to seek clarification and understanding even if it shows she "doesn't know," has been a cornerstone of Stephanie's success (and is a cornerstone of all creative leaders' success: the idea that it is okay to sit with and manage uncertainty until a single or multiple possible answers or ideas emerge). It has allowed her to navigate the complex and often unpredictable world of Hollywood and has shown, as Socrates informed us millennia ago, that asking good questions in the face of uncertainty is probably the most important and underutilized skill in the world today.

Stephanie emphasizes that by doing this, by leading by example through questions and curiosity about creative matters, it gives her people permission to follow suit. "When your team sees you being curious and exploring new ideas, they feel empowered to do the same," she told us. "Leadership is really about creating a safe space where curiosity is celebrated, questions are asked, and everyone feels comfortable sharing their thoughts and ideas and not like they are going to be judged, ignored, or shunned for going out on a limb."

Stephanie's curiosity also extends to the area of problem-solving (one of the main features of a producer's job) specifically regarding being transparent and forthcoming if there is a problem. She told us, "When you're working with a client, you should do everything you can to solve a problem before you go to them. I'm a big believer in not being a problem bringer-upper, but being a problem solver. I try not to go into a client's office and say I have a problem about X,Y and Z, and now I'm making it your problem. Instead, I try to tell them about the problem,and that I'm really struggling because X,Y, and Z happened. But then I also want to explain how I solved it. Depending upon the situation, I may want to hear if they thought I did it the right way, or I might share three solutions I've come up with and ask their opinion on which solution they think is best or might be most effective. So I try to use this approach when I communicate up the chain of command: this is the problem that we're facing and here are the solutions that we've come up with or the solution I've chosen and I want to make sure you're comfortable with that."

Stephanie's problem-solving approach reflects a proactive and curious mindset. Instead of merely presenting problems, she seeks to understand them deeply and come up with potential different solutions that various stakeholders would be comfortable with. "It's what drives us to keep pushing the envelope and delivering fresh, engaging stories even in the face of obstacles."

By asking questions, seeking to understand, and exploring new possibilities, Stephanie Drachkovitch has carved a unique and successful path in Hollywood on the back of her curiosity.

Key Takeaways:

1. **Curiosity Drives Breakthroughs**: Throughout history, from Nobel Prize winners to Hollywood producers like Spielberg and Cameron, curiosity has been a common trait linked to major innovations and creative achievements. It opens new avenues for exploration and problem-solving.

2. **Dangers of Hyper-Specialization**: The prevailing "SAT Ideology" emphasizing hyper-specialization can limit creativity and problem-solving abilities. Overly specialized in-

dividuals often miss broader perspectives and fail to adapt in a rapidly changing world.

3. **Impact on Leadership**: Leaders who encourage curiosity and diversity of thought tend to foster more innovative and adaptable teams. Micromanagers and control-oriented leaders, on the other hand, stifle creativity, reduce morale, and hinder organizational effectiveness.

4. **Cultivating Curiosity**: Practical strategies for cultivating curiosity include asking deeper questions, exposing oneself to diverse experiences and perspectives, and adopting a growth mindset focused on continuous learning and adaptation.

5. **Curiosity in Action**: Examples like Stephanie Drachkovitch wondering if there could be a show in an anecdote she heard on television and her determination to pursue an idea that hadn't been done before demonstrate how curiosity can lead to unexpected successes and breakthroughs, even in industries resistant to change.

CHAPTER 3

I'LL HAVE THAT WITH A SIDE OF OPTIMISM

"Optimism is a strategy for making a better future. Because unless you believe that the future can be better, you are unlikely to step up and take responsibility for making it so."
— **Noam Chomsky**

A leader's mood, personality, and outlook will make or break entire team performances. According to countless studies, for example, a leader's mood is like an emotional contagion spreading far and wide and will re-create the emotions they are personally experiencing in their followers—a psychological and physiological phenomenon we will explore in more depth in the next chapter. But suffice it to say for now, what you need to know is that up to 70% of any organization's emotional environment is determined by a single leader.[2]

This emotional leadership contagion is made far more interesting and consequential when inserted into the classic debate on whether a leader should be realistic, pessimistic, or optimistic. And while this debate has usually started and ended in the context of how each of these outlooks impact overall team performance, it is far more nuanced than just influencing outcomes.

Harry Friedman, the 19-time Emmy® Award Winning producer of over 5,000 episodes of *Jeopardy!*, told us,

"There is no place in my world for pessimism or pessimistic people. For years I sported a baseball cap from the *Life Is Good* line that depicts a half glass of water and the caption Half Full. I have often reminded my team that our shows are meant to be fun and it's really okay…no, really encouraged…to have fun doing it. We should always take our work seriously but not ourselves."

But why does Harry have such a strong bias against pessimism? Is it just a personal preference? Is it the type of show he ran? Or is there something more to his creative leadership philosophy than his own circumstantial factors?

Turns out, Harry acutely understands that pessimism in leaders causes them to be perceived as less effective by their teams.[3] He also acutely understands that pessimism leads to reduced team morale, motivation, and trust, and diminishes creativity, collaboration, and problem-solving abilities based on numerous empirical studies.[4,5] Put differently, it turns out Harry intuitively knows—and knows by experience—that pessimism is the least practical and least effective leadership strategy there is, and the most counterproductive one at that.

But you might be objecting and saying that there are plenty of pessimistic—or fear based—leaders out there, and their ability to climb to the top seems almost ubiquitous. While we grant this point, and also grant the point that there are even historical leaders who were pessimistic like Stalin, Nixon, and Neville Chamberlain (the British Prime Minister who appeased Hitler instead of standing up to him) who sometimes made it to the top, we stand firm in the data that their impact on others and the future often result in failure, humiliation, and backlash. Just because Machiavelli (another pessimistic leader) said it was better to be feared (i.e., produce pessimism and dread in your followers) than loved doesn't mean he was right; in fact, he was dead wrong based on the most cutting edge and wide ranging modern scientific scholarship of how to lead teams. Why? Because they would be committing the "5 Dysfunctions of a Team" as outlined in Patrick Lenconi's seminal book of the same name: inducing a dysfunctional environment that reflected the absence of trust, a fear of conflict, a lack of commitment, avoidance of accountability, and inattention to results.[6] All because of pessimism.

Harry bookended this idea by telling us:

"Nothing is a greater threat to productivity and creativity than a production office or a set that gives off a bad vibe. Effective leadership still means setting the right tone and leading by example."

The Role of Being "Realistic" in Leadership

But you might also be wondering about the next level up from pessimism: having a realistic outlook about leadership. After all, it's better not to get everyone's hopes up and be disappointed in the end, right?

Well, this turns out to be the wrong approach too. Why? Because projecting only realism on to a team produces nearly similar effects in, and results for, team members and their performance.[7]

For example, leaders who are overly realistic often struggle to inspire and motivate their teams, leading to reduced enthusiasm and creativity. Leaders who are overly realistic also frequently fail to pursue ambitious goals, are too risk averse, and miss numerous growth opportunities for their organizations according to research.[8] This is one of the reasons why professional sports coaches, even if they have a losing record and all of the odds against them, never tell their teams before a game, "The truth is we are probably going to lose. The other team is just too big, too fast, too strong, and so much better. So don't even think about winning because it's not going to happen." However, many traditional leaders' convey this very message to their teams by trying to be "realistic" often without even realizing it. This outlook—whether conscious or subconscious—can reduce performance by as much as 25% according to studies.[9]

Optimistic Leadership

Producer Fanshen Giovanni Cox, whose story we will explore more later in the book, told us, "Honestly, why would anyone want to produce or lead without optimism? Why do it at all if you can't do it right?"

She has a point. Optimism in creative leaders, unlike realism or pessimism, is the most effective outlook to have. It accomplishes the following:

- Enhances positive emotions in team members and provides psychological safety (the belief that one will not be judged or humiliated for speaking up with ideas, concerns, or mistakes in a work or group environment)[10]

- Improves creative thinking and problem-solving abilities[11]

- Promotes resilience in the face of setbacks[12]

- Substantially increases productivity and goal attainment[13]

- Increases financial success[14]

- Enhances mental, emotional, and even physical health in teams and organizations[15]

Continuing with our sports coaching analogy from above, for example, studies have shown that the coaches at the most elite levels possessed optimism as their primary leadership outlook (not pessimism or realism). Of course, they were also demanding and had high standards, but they coupled that with believing they could get the best performances out of their teams.

The same is true of Hollywood producers and creative leaders more generally. In their cases, just as in the case of sports coaches, it's incredibly important because they are at a disadvantage compared to traditional leaders. And that disadvantage is found in the more negative and challenging mental and emotional makeup of their teams. Put differently, high achievers in the sporting, artistic, and creative fields tend to experience more negative emotions, battle with mood disorders and neuroticism at a much higher rate than the general population, and have difficulty letting go of perfectionism. So coaches and producers, as a rule, must be optimistic so they can pass this energy and emotion on to their performers who might otherwise get trapped in self-doubt and paralysis, undermining their performance and the overall team goal.

All of this said, there is a significant caveat to mention here: optimism has its limits. Producer Arthur Smith, who is also the author of the phenomenal book *Reach: Hard Lessons and Learned Truths from a Lifetime in Television*, told us,

"There's a danger to being overly optimistic, because that means everything is going great and that just doesn't happen on television. There's also a danger to being overly pessimistic because it's just a downer and all you're thinking about is what could go wrong. The right stance is to hope for the best, but plan for the worst."

What Arthur is highlighting, and so many of our other Hollywood producers told us, is not to put blinders on as a leader. Not to be Pollyanna-ish when it comes to planning, preparation, and being caught off guard. They told us that it is better to be hopeful, which is defined as having an optimistic but clear goal with a clear pathway to get there, knowing that there will be bumps in the road along the way. But this hope is not based on blind faith optimism—it believes for the best (optimism), plans for the worst (pessimism), and expects that things will turn out better than average (which is realism). So you can say, creative leadership is heavily optimistic with a healthy dose of realism (that is downplayed but still prepared for). A good book that explores this healthy dose of optimistic reality is *Leadership and Self-Deception: Getting out of the Box* by The Arbinger Institute[16].

Becoming More Optimistic and Hopeful As a Creative Leader

But regardless of where you currently stand in terms of your personal propensity toward optimism, pessimism, or realism, it is possible to become as realistically optimistic as possible. By the way, if you want a scientifically valid way to see how prone you are to optimism versus pessimism, you might want want to check out the "BIG 5" personality test and see where you land on neuroticism, which will give you a scale of how prone you are toward looking at things negatively or positively.[17] In the meantime, here are a few simple ways to become more optimistic than you are today:

1. **Practice focusing on 3 things you're grateful for that happened today (and do this every day).** This will help you look on the bright side of things, and research shows that when you do this for several weeks in a row, your positive emotions and optimism will skyrocket.[18] But the caveat here is to say these 3 things out loud and to slow down your thoughts enough so that you can feel (and imagine in your mind's eye) what you're grateful for as you say them. In other words, don't rush it, but savor the moment by re-experiencing what you're grateful for.

2. **Practice positive self-talk.** Speaking positive words out loud to yourself will activate neurochemicals like dopamine and serotonin, which will in turn strengthen the neu-

ral networks of your brain responsible for optimism (and a host of other things). If you employ the research-backed tool the "Losada Rule," which is to speak at least 3 positive words for every negative or neutral word you speak, you can accelerate the changing of your brain and positivity outlook. And while this is not a formula, you can nonetheless experiment with the number of positive to negative words spoken, though preferably you want to be biased toward positive[19].

3. **Focus on celebrating regular team progress, not simply recognizing specific team members once they've achieved a goal.** Studies show that employees are both happier and more productive when they feel like they are *celebrated while* they make meaningful progress toward a goal, and not just celebrated for something they've achieved after the fact.[20] While this might seem counterintuitive, encouraging your team while they are making progressive gains can leave them feeling energized and motivated in a more sustainable way—and it will make you come off as a more optimistic leader since you are emphasizing the importance of the journey with them and not just the importance of the destination.

4. **Professionally invest in your self care.** Seeing a nutritionist, physical trainer, sleep expert, and a Solutions-Focused Therapist (who invests in building your greatest virtues and strengths) will allow you to optimize your life in a way so that you are building the mental, emotional, and physical resources and capacities to be more optimistic than you are today.[21] Of course, you can always employ the D-I-Y approach, but experts can put you on a more accelerated path that can create profound transformations in you and your leadership.

CASE STUDY: HARRY FRIEDMAN'S LEADERSHIP SECRET: THE POWER OF OPTIMISM

Harry Friedman, the iconic producer behind *Jeopardy!* and a personal recipient of 19 Emmy® Awards, embodies the essence of leadership optimism. With over 9,000 episodes of television along with 100 Emmy® nominations under his belt, his approach to leadership has not only shaped the shows' success but also offers priceless lessons for leaders across industries. Harry's philosophy revolves around maintaining a positive outlook, fostering a collaborative environment, and leading with empathy and clarity.

But Harry's journey to mastering the art and science of optimistic leadership wasn't without its challenges. He recalls a particularly chaotic day during the production of *Hollywood Squares,* another show he produced. "It turns out that on a particular *Hollywood Squares* tape day, we lost two celebrities, so I had to replace them within a matter of hours. So I called impressionist Rich Little and I said, 'Rich, could you come in and do the show this afternoon? I need you to be yourself and two other people.' And he did. We put him on the top row. He jumped around from one square to the other depending on which one was called. And we never knew who he was going to be. He gave us some guidelines of his favorites, which were Reagan and Nixon, and it worked out. It was a lesson in problem-solving that I didn't know that I needed to learn."

This incident was more than just a story of quick thinking; it was an example of the power of optimism in leadership. Where others might have seen this as an insurmountable problem—and canceled the shoot and lost lots of money or even their job (these sorts of things happen frequently in Hollywood)—Harry saw an opportunity for creativity and collaboration. His unwavering belief that things would work out, even in the face of adversity, not only saved the day but also set a tone for his team that "if something could go right, it would" (the opposite of *Murphy's Law* that states "if something can go wrong, it will"). This "overcoming" approach in the face of all obstacles, rooted in optimism, would become a hallmark of his leadership style throughout the years. Perhaps we can think of it as "Harry's Law."

One of Harry's core principles was to never criticize or correct an employee in front of others. He believed that such actions were demoralizing and counterproductive. Instead, he advocated for addressing issues privately and constructively. "Have a vision for what you want to do, but always have a plan B. Be open to ideas from others and credit them publicly if their idea is implemented. It doesn't diminish you in any way and builds morale. If their idea doesn't work, talk to them about it privately and under no circumstances embarrass them," Harry advised.

This human element is part of what made Harry so successful. "Learn people's names. Nothing will endear a boss faster to an employee than calling the employee by name. 'Hey buddy' just doesn't cut it," he told us. "Never be unkind. Lead by example. Be clear in your directives and in outlining roles and responsibilities," Harry further told us. "Admit when you don't know something, learn how to read the room, and don't step over dollars to get dimes."

No truer words could be spoken. Harry's wisdom encapsulates the essence of his creative leadership philosophy, one that emphasizes optimism, humility, and a human-centered approach, things all creative leaders should focus on. He also told us one last thing creative leaders should focus on: "Remember, you want to always strive for the 3 R's. Revenue is one, Ratings is another, but the most important one is Relationships."

Key Takeaways

1. **Leader's Emotional Impact**: A leader's mood significantly influences team dynamics through emotional contagion, affecting up to 70% of an organization's emotional climate. Optimistic leaders can inspire positivity and resilience, whereas pessimistic leaders may dampen morale and creativity.

2. **Impact of Pessimism**: Pessimistic leaders, like those in historical contexts such as Stalin or Nixon, often create environments marked by distrust, fear of conflict, and low commitment. Studies indicate pessimism can reduce team performance by up to 25%, emphasizing its counterproductive nature.

3. **Realism vs. Optimism**: While realism is often seen as a balanced perspective, overly realistic leaders may struggle to motivate teams towards ambitious goals, leading to missed opportunities and reduced creativity. Optimism, on the other hand, enhances positive emotions, creativity, and goal attainment.

4. **Optimistic Leadership Benefits**: Optimistic leaders like Harry Friedman of "Jeopardy!" foster environments that encourage fun, creativity, and high morale. Optimism promotes psychological safety, resilience in adversity, and overall team success, backed by empirical evidence across various fields.

5. **Balanced Optimism**: Effective leaders combine optimism with a pragmatic approach that acknowledges potential challenges (realism) while maintaining hope and

positivity. This balanced approach fosters a resilient team culture that can weather setbacks while striving for ambitious goals.

CHAPTER 4

WHO SAID YOU HAVE TO PLAY IN THE SANDBOX?

"Play is the highest form of research."[1]
— **N.V. Scarfe**

"When you are playful and having fun, you are more likely to perform better and find creative solutions."
— **Shawn Achor**

One of the biggest differentiators between a traditional leader and a creative one is the amount each emphasizes on play. On having fun. On seeking to solve problems with not only outside of the box thinking, but of blowing up the box metaphor altogether.

Whereas a traditional leader might hold mistaken misconceptions about play—that it is unprofessional, just fun and games, for certain industries only, time-wasting, or just for extroverts—creative leaders embrace the true science of it: that it works, and that it works more effectively than "serious" leadership does according to countless studies.

For example, here is what empirical data says about "serious" or traditional leadership:

- It suppresses creativity[2]

- It reduces employee engagement and job satisfaction[3]

- It increases employee turnover rates[4]

- It creates communication barriers and negative organizational culture[5]

- It diminishes trust[6]

- It impairs decision making[7]

- It reduces overall performance, including financial performance[8]

Clearly, the drawbacks are significant. And even if a serious leader thinks they're inspiring their team to perform using leadership classics like *The Art of War*, *The 48 Laws of Power*, and *Winning*, they are inadvertently thwarting their own effectiveness.[9][10][11] Why? Because healthy leadership is not about dominating or manipulating others (and making them miserable) for short-term results; it is about empowering and supporting others in an uplifting environment so that, collectively, everyone can be their best and do their best over the long-term. Unfortunately, only 19% of employees surveyed by Deloitte across various firms believe they have the types of leaders or workplace cultures that allow them to thrive.[12] This might be because their leaders believe the "one right way" to lead doesn't involve having playful fun—or any fun at all.

Producer Jonathan Murray, who you met earlier, thinks that many leaders do their best to be "Little Napoleons" because they fear they won't be respected or get the job done if they change their approach and reveal their humanity. Jonathan told us about the false understanding leaders throughout the country promote this idea,

"It's wrong to think you can't show vulnerability as a leader…and I don't think that's true. I think you can because I don't think vulnerability is a weakness. I think you have to let your staff know that you're real too, and that you have vulnerabilities, which gives them room to have vulnerabilities and to share if they're having challenges…It doesn't mean you can't be a decisive leader even though you can be vulnerable. It doesn't mean that you can't make tough decisions if you're vulnerable. It just means that maybe you have some humanity about what you're doing."

This fear that many leaders have of showing their vulnerability is perhaps one of the biggest reasons more of them don't emphasize play at work (or even act like humans in some cases). Whether they have been taught incorrectly at school, observed bosses who led incorrectly by trying to pretend to be macho, have a major case of imposter-syndrome, or some other barrier to making work more fun.

For example, books like Play: *How it Shapes the Brain, Opens the Imagination, and Invigorates the Soul* by Dr. Stuart Brown and *Playful Leadership: How to Enable Fearless Organizational Cultures and Boost Your Bottom Line* by Chris Edwards and Mark McKegrow go into incredible depth about the specifics for how to do this.[13,14] We will also offer a few specific tips shortly so you can turbocharge play in your own creative leadership as well, which reports show approximately 80% of employees crave more, and which result in 21% higher profits.[15 16] According to world class research, when you make play central, the benefits include the following:

- Enhanced workplace creativity and problem-solving[17]

- Stronger team trust, collaboration, and communication[18]

- Better attraction of top talent and retaining of top talent[19]

- Higher employee satisfaction, stress reduction, and improved conflict resolution skills[20]

- Increased productivity and performance[21]

- And more adaptable leadership to navigate uncertainty, crises, and new opportunities[22]

Harry Friedman told us about how remaining playful—and therefore adaptable to any situation that might arise—helped him during a challenging taping of *Wheel of Fortune* that nobody could have expected. He said,

"We were doing a celebrity week on *Wheel of Fortune*. And one of the celebrities was William Shatner. And after the first commercial break in his episode, he motioned me to come over and he said, "I have to leave now." And I said, "The restrooms are nearby. So we can certainly wait for you." He said, "No, no, no, I have to leave." I said, "But we're not finished with the show." He responded, "But I have a flight to catch. So I'm going now." And he left. Now, fortunately, we always have a standby celebrity and it was the only time we ever had to use that fallback position. It was Julie Pinson from *General Hospital*. We came back from a commercial break and Pat Sajak just simply said, "Hey, Bill Shatner, we thank you for being here, and stepping in at the red position is our friend Julie Pinson from *General Hospital*, Julie, it's your turn. Spin the wheel." So thank God for Pat. Thank God for Julie."

In this case, Harry didn't freak out; Pat Sajak didn't worry how it would make him look by welcoming back Bill Shatner and then having Julia Pinson take his place; and the show didn't receive any negative repercussions in the ratings or revenue for this episode. Yes, viewers noticed the change up, but they took it in a good natured stride as well.

Part of the reason it worked so well is because while creative leaders like Harry demand excellence, they forgo the deadly idea that perfection is even possible. Perfection, to these incredibly successful leaders, is like chasing a shadow that doesn't exist; not only is it an illusion, but it creates all of the drawbacks of serious leadership mentioned earlier. Of course, perfection is needed in life and death scenarios—something Harry will talk about later in the book—but most scenarios aren't life or death in leadership. Even if they are, the benefits of having a playful mindset like adaptability and improved creative problem solving and decision making still make you a better leader. Even in moments of crisis, or on a handful of specific things like ethical dilemmas, disciplinary actions, and the like, you can find ways to integrate play into your leadership.

Outside of Hollywood, leaders have proven time and time again that they can use this playful approach to make work more fun—and successful. For example, Richard Branson, the Founder and former CEO of Virgin, famously participated in hot air balloon rides and would race Formula One race cars against other executives to add excitement and attention to his company.[23,24] Herb Kelleher, the former CEO of Southwest Airlines, would regularly have arm wrestling matches with his employees and have dress up and costume days to keep things light and everyone engaged.[25] And Joe Coulombe, of Trader Joes, would encourage his workers to wear Hawaiin shirts, quirkily design their stores, and create fun item names to products (like "Two-Buck Chuck" to wine) to attract customers to the most unusual and fun grocery store out there.[26]

Producer Allison Grodner also emphasized that she likes to keep things warm, playful, and fun on her sets. She told us,

"This could just be my, you know, Jewish nature but it's my pet peeve that people have to have food on my set; people have to be fed. If we don't have enough food or the food is late, I might actually yell about that. When the crew is taking a break I get so anxious; I really feel that we work in a wide range of budgets and conditions, especially in unscripted television, and so I can't always promise you're getting paid top dollar because it's just not possible, but I want to make sure that you have a good time, that you're treated well, and that you're well fed."

What's striking here is that although the entertainment industry is known for paying top dollar in some cases, it is not always the case. But Allison has still been able to attract the top talent for projects that were not higher budget, because she developed a well deserved reputation for joyous sets with lots of food. These intangibles, which are difficult to explain in traditional leadership algorithms, can go a long way. As the 10 x NCAA national championship basketball coach John Wooden—who also wrote various books on leadership, which highlighted his famous "Pyramid of Success"—said: "It's the little details that are vital. Little things make big things happen."[27] Interestingly enough, Wooden was so focused on little details that the first exercise he would teach his new players was the proper way to put on socks—an infinitesimally small detail that doesn't seem to matter at all but which many of his players realized was a key to their unparalleled success: doing all of the little things most everyone else takes for granted that, taken together, gave them untold competitive advantages.[28]

Science-Based Strategies to Increase Your Playfulness at Work

Our producers, and even John Wooden, emphasized the importance of play, fun, and small intangible details in a way that makes the scientific studies and statistics come alive. They also emphasized that these things can be learned.

Academy Award winning producer Andrew Carlberg told us,

"I encourage everyone to read, watch, and experience as much as you can because that's the fun part of your job…and so you're having to continually self-educate as much as you can."

And if companies outside of Hollywood like Etsy, IDEO, and Hubspot taught themselves how to play, so can yours. Here are a few tips backed by the top empirical data:

1. **Playful leadership is done best by example.** By being open to spontaneity, using appropriate humor, and engaging in light hearted banter and activities, you can set a more positive and playful tone for your team.[29]

2. **Create playful workspaces.** Installing more color, vibrant plants, art-filled corridors, chalkboard walls, and the like will boost the playfulness of your office. And while you don't need game rooms, air hockey tables, and other amenities like Silicon Valley giants, spicing up your decor even modestly can improve the fun vibe.[30]

3. **Flex time and experimentation.** 3M created it and Google perfected it: allocating a certain amount of time to employees to experiment with their own projects or even with novel approaches toward company projects that may be different than or outside the norm; allowing freedom to explore will make people more creative and playful. And in the cases of 3M and Google, the Post-It Note, Sandpaper, Google Maps, Gmail, and Google Chrome all came out of employee's "spare time" when they were just "playing around."[31,32]

4. **Promote collaborative play and regular team building activities.** Whether team sports, puzzle solving challenges, improv exercises, or the like, these collaborative play sessions should be done regularly—monthly or bimonthly even, not just during company retreats or leadership or wellness training.[33]

5. **Promote gamified learning and interactive workshops.** By providing continued professional development using more playful trainers, curriculum, or technology, your team will always want to continue learning more to help boost your own organizational effectiveness because they will equate it with fun .They will not see professional

development as a chore, as so many corporate trainings are seen—and often are.[34]

6. **Promote regular creativity and brainstorming sessions.** By spitballing ideas continuously without judgment or reprisal, team members will enjoy generating new ideas and potential solutions in a playful way. Some of your best ideas from perhaps even unknown sources within your organization can contribute in a way that could be stimulating not only for them as an experience, but also potentially profitable for you if the idea is good and you implement it successfully.[35]

These are just a few ways for how to work on your own playfulness, but they are doable, can be low cost, and are essential to grow in your own creative leadership capabilities.

CASE STUDY: LLOYD J. SCHWARTZ'S PLAYBOOK: TURNING PLAY INTO BUSINESS SUCCESS

Lloyd J. Schwartz, a revered Hollywood producer of *The Brady Bunch* fame among many other classic shows, embodies the essence of playful, creative leadership. Known for his original and empathetic leadership style, Lloyd understands that success isn't about making overwhelming and unreasonable demands on people or completing projects with an iron fist—or by any means necessary—as many traditional leaders do. Instead, he believes it's about inspiring and engaging a team in a way that allows them to flourish, both personally and professionally, while having fun along the way.

For instance, Lloyd told us about a particularly demanding shoot one day, where tensions were running high. But instead of succumbing to the stress by yelling and screaming, cursing others, or panicking about the situation, which is very easy for many leaders to do in these circumstances (and also the wrong thing to do according to mountainous scientific data), he turned the situation around with a simple yet powerful act of playfulness. He organized an impromptu pizza party for the crew, which wound up transforming the tense atmosphere into one of camaraderie and joy. As a result, the crew's morale immediately improved and their creativity kicked back into high gear, which demonstrates how play can positively impact mood and how mood, in turn, can positively impact performance.

Among Lloyd's many stories about his playful approach to his work, he told us another one about a seemingly trivial request that his famous producer father (the creator of *Gilligan's*

Island) asked him to do: to "go run a looping session." Fresh in his producer role as a young 20-something, Lloyd faced a dilemma: he knew nothing about what a "looping session" entailed. Yet, his response was classic Schwartz: he said, "Right away sir." He didn't say this because he was familiar with the term or knew anything about what the process meant; he said it because he was determined to learn and to do so with an optimistic (and some would even say fake-it-till-you-make-it) spirit. As he stepped into Paramount Studios to do this looping session, he walked to the stage where an actor was engaged in what is known as dialogue replacement—something he had never witnessed before. With a bank of dials and beeps filling the room, Lloyd's initial anxiety transformed into an opportunity to learn—and test his own playful leadership style.

When the looping session technician turned to him after a take and asked him, "How was that, sir?" Lloyd's answer was both a challenge and a revelation: "The only thing you could say in a situation like that, because I didn't know whether it was good or not, was: 'it's not good enough,' which made us do multiple takes so I could learn what was actually good and what wasn't."

After many experiences like this, and after decades of successful television shows, musicals, plays, books, and the like, Lloyd put his playful leadership approach in writing. Or, as he likes to call this, he put it into his 'Hollywood Truisms.' They are here for your indulgence:

1. If someone says, "Trust me." Don't.

2. If someone says, "I'm telling you this for your own good." It isn't.

3. If someone says, "I'm telling you this as a friend." They're not. They're not a friend, and they're not telling you this as a friend. (Were they ever at your house for a barbecue? Then they're not your friend.)

4. Worst case scenario is the scenario.

5. Fall back position is the position.

6. If there is a 99% chance that something is going to happen, there is a 100% chance that it won't happen. If someone says "We're starting Monday," it means we're not starting Monday or Tuesday or ever.

7. If you're invited to a meeting at a certain time, and everybody else is already there and talking, it's not good for you.

8. If at the end of a meeting, someone says to someone else, "Can I talk to you for a minute?" And they're not saying it to you, it's not good for you.

9. If people tell you it's better that you're not at a meeting, it's certain that it's not better for you, and only better for them.

10. If you've been involved with a project, and now they're not calling you, and they tell you that nothing is happening. Something is happening, and it's happening to you.

11. "Keeping you apprised" is the same thing as "keeping you removed."

12. "Can I get right back to you?" means you will never hear from them again.

13. "Let's have lunch," means let's not have lunch.

14. "Can we postpone lunch again?" means there will never be a lunch.

15. "We're still thinking about it" means they don't remember you and/or your project.

16. If someone says it's transparent, it's only transparent if he or she is doing the looking. When you look, it's opaque.

17. If someone thanks you for your patience, they are thanking you for letting them screw you.

18. If a company says that they are so happy to be working with you, it means they are glad you haven't figured out how they're screwing you. The same is true if they call you a team player.

19. The check is in the mail means there will never be a check.

20. If they say the money is about to come in means there never was any money.

21. If they say, we're waiting for offices, there never will be offices.

22. If a company or a producer or a casting director describes you or a script as interesting it means they are not interested.

Key Takeaways

1. **The Power of Play**: Play is not just frivolous; it's a powerful tool that galvanizes creativity, problem-solving, and overall performance. Research, including insights from Albert Einstein and Shawn Achor, emphasizes that playful environments cultivate better solutions and higher levels of achievement.

2. **Misconceptions about Play**: Traditional leaders often view play as unprofessional or time-wasting. However, empirical data reveals that a lack of play can suppress creativity, diminish employee engagement, and create negative organizational cultures, ultimately undermining long-term success.

3. **Benefits of Playful Leadership**: Embracing play in leadership leads to numerous benefits. It enhances workplace creativity, deepens team trust and communication, attracts and retains talent, improves employee satisfaction, reduces stress, and boosts productivity. Examples from industries like entertainment underscore how playfulness can lead to unexpected solutions and maintain positive morale.

4. **Practical Strategies for Playful Leadership**: Implementing playful leadership involves leading by example, creating vibrant workspaces, allowing flexible work arrangements for experimentation, organizing regular team-building activities, incorporating gamified learning, and designing creative brainstorming sessions. These strategies not only enhance workplace dynamics but also stimulate innovation and adaptive thinking among teams.

5. **Cultural Impact**: Cultivating a playful work culture necessitates overcoming barriers like fear of vulnerability and outdated leadership paradigms. Leaders who embrace play alongside seriousness create environments where teams thrive, leveraging the benefits of both structured goals and spontaneous creativity.

CHAPTER 5

ONCE UPON A STORY

"The universe is made of stories, not of atoms."
— **Muriel Rukeyser**

In addition to curiosity, optimism, and play, one of the greatest tools in any creative leader's arsenal is storytelling. Stories provide not only entertainment for employees, but they also bring inspiration, education, and motivation.[2-4]

It's no wonder then that, from the beginning of recorded history, stories have been the primary way identity, values, purpose, and belonging have been communicated, and the greatest leaders of all time are often remembered for their incredible storytelling abilities. When people think about Lincoln, King, or Churchill, for example, what immediately comes to mind? Their stories (as told through their speeches). When people think of Mandela, Disney, or Richard Branson, what instantly comes to mind? Their stories (as told in a variety of ways).

Likewise, when people think of a particular leader or organization, they often think of a story—either the story the leader or the organization has told and cultivated, or the story that people have told themselves about that leader or organization (for better or for worse).

In other words, although facts, figures, and logic are important things to have, they are secondary to storytelling as far as a creative leader's ability to foster an impression and persuade others to acknowledge it. Story is King, as they say in Hollywood, and it is also king everywhere else.

Allison Grodner, the producer of 25 seasons of the hit series *Big Brother*, told us about the importance of storytelling. In particular, she shared a story she uses to teach her team not what to think or do in specific ethical dilemmas, but to help them raise important questions and ponder the deeper implications of their work (that sometimes doesn't have easy Yes or No answers) to unexpected challenges that pop up. She said,

"I did a documentary many years ago for HBO called *Small Town Ecstasy*, and it was under Sheila Nevins. It was set out to be a documentary about rave culture and drugs and ecstasy. And we went out to a number of raves and all of that, a very small crew.

"We ultimately stumbled upon a person in his late thirties or early forties at the time; it was so strange because there were a lot of younger kids, and then there was this guy and he was newly divorced and what appeared to be in a midlife crisis and was involved in rave culture. His older adult son had gotten him into it during this time and so he was dropping ecstasy and so forth. And so that became our story. We had to find how we were gonna document this, what our narrative would be, and then we found him and it just tumbled from there because we caught him during this insane time.

"We were following him for a number of weeks and discovered he had some younger kids. They were in their early teens or tweens, and they were at a rave with him. Our crew was there, our producer and director were there, but I wasn't there physically. But then one day they told me that his kids want to take ecstasy and he's letting him. And I thought to myself, "Oh crap, I was never trained for this. What in the world should we do?

"I remember going, wow, this is one of those ethical crises right now, because we have this amazing story and it's about to go terribly wrong and yet there's the moral obligation to these minors. But he's their parent and he's allowing this and it was all happening very quickly—it wasn't like he was asking our permission to let them take ecstasy.

As a documentarian, you are supposed to be a "fly on the wall" and not interfere. It was clear, our subjects were going to do what they were going to do whether we were there or not. But this is where it was tough: being a human being and a mom, I thought we must be the responsible adults in the room and be able to intervene in an emergency. It was a tough one—do you interfere with your subjects, which you are not supposed to do in a documentary? It's a really tough call. Obviously, my team called me and I had hoped I had made the right decision.

"It's really interesting how it unfolded because the mom found out about what happened when the kids were with their father. And she ended up taking her ex-husband to court. We were still filming when all of this happened so the documentary was able to capture the consequences of his actions. This man's children banded together and decided to do an intervention to help their father and to stop him from doing drugs. It was very emotional and he ultimately agreed to get the help he needed."

We were both at the edge of our seats when Allison told us this story. What would we have done in that scenario? What would you have done? And this story illustrates exactly how a story compellingly told can be far more captivating and get us to think long and hard about certain things in a way facts or logic might not.

Your Brain on Stories

There is a scientific reason for why all of us become so enthralled when we hear stories like Allison's, which we will finish in a bit. The short answer is because we are biologically wired for it.[5]

For example, stories ignite the parts of our brain associated with "neural coupling" and "mirror neurons," which means this: the emotions the storyteller is conveying in their tales are instantly awakened in us.[6][7] Put differently, we feel what the storyteller is feeling, we feel what their characters are feeling, and we put ourselves in their shoes—without even realizing it. This is why you might cry every time Mufassa dies in *The Lion King*, feel scared watching *Scream*, laugh out loud at feel good movies like The Rock's *Jumanji*, or feel inspired when the President is giving his speech against the alien invaders in *Independence Day*.

Ample brain research has been conducted around this phenomenon. One of the more interesting findings is that the neurochemicals released through the storyteller or their characters are released into us too.[8] So if they are feeling joy and peace (and experiencing the neurochemicals dopamine and serotonin), we feel the same; if they are feeling anger and disgust (and experiencing the neurochemical cortisol), we are feeling the same. This is what it means that the neurons are mirroring: we are reflecting back the same physiological and emotional reactions as them.

The same thing is true with other physiological reactions in our bodies besides neurochemicals. In a 2021 experimental research project by Melanie C. Green and her team, for example, researchers recruited a diverse population of people to measure how psychologically and physiologically close they felt to characters in film clips they were shown.[9] They asked participants to give self-reports on their emotional reaction to clips. They also measured participants' physiological reactions like heart rate. What they found was that, depending on which emotion the storyteller was trying to manipulate or evoke, the participant would feel the emotion and not only report it, but their physiology would report it too; the storyteller could strongly influence what is going on in the physical hearts of their audience.

But stories don't just invoke emotions. They also become more memorable than facts presented in isolation, are easier to cognitively understand, and are far more persuasive to the brain and heart in terms of influencing behavior. They also bypass our brain's natural anti-persuasion systems, which automatically kick in whenever we feel somebody is trying to persuade us using facts and figures. This is true not only with Hollywood stories, but also is true in all good stories told outside of Hollywood.

Benefits of Storytelling in Creative Leadership

Truth be told, the greatest benefit of storytelling is not just because they're persuasive instruments; it's because they inspire others into (hopefully positive) action. Unlike traditional leaders who often rely on transactional interactions, fear, or data to tell their subordinates what to do, creative leaders motivate others by appealing to the best things inside of them.

Arthur Smith, the Executive Producer of *American Ninja Warrior*, who you will meet more a little later, told us a story about how he was able to inspire the executives at NBC to take action and launch *The Titan Games* starring Dwayne "The Rock" Johnson. And why did he have to inspire them? These great execs needed to be sure that the show would be different from *American Ninja Warrior* and different from the other competition shows out there.

Arthur told us,

"For the *Titan Games* we were in development with NBC for a long time. NBC had come to me because *American Ninja Warrior* was a hit and they asked, "What's the next physical competition show?" We wanted to do something that felt fresh and original, so we developed a competition show we called *Hercules* with Greek mythology as a through line.

Everything changed when we identified a talent that we wanted to attach: Dwayne "The Rock" Johnson. I had finally sold NBC on *Hercules*; we already had the deal on that. But once we identified Dwayne "The Rock" Johnson as the perfect partner and talent on the project, everything changed. I thought about what he was doing on social media and how he was inspiring people. He went from a football player who got cut to becoming a superhero. And I said, 'We're gonna take regular people and make them superheroes.'

Let that last line sink in: "we're going to take regular people and make them superheroes." This thinking, this type of storytelling (in the form of a single sentence in this case), was enough to inspire NBC to take Arthur's show out of development (the very long Hollywood process where a show is being worked on but still has a slim shot of ever filming or airing) and greenlight it.

But why does inspirational storytelling work so well? Why does it benefit the creative leader so much? How does it work even on people who work in stories for a living like the professionals in Hollywood?

Well, studies have shown the remarkable advantages of stories. For example, Forbes and Harvard Business Review have documented that leaders who use storytelling are perceived as up to 70% more effective than those who don't [10, 11]; they are 22 x more likely to remember a fact wrapped in a story versus a fact presented on its own [12]; they increase engagement by 300% when a story is presented [13]; and they improve organizational change initiatives by making them 2000% more likely to succeed when storytelling is used as inspiration [14].

Clearly the benefits are enormous both for the leader and their team and organization. Their ability to increase engagement, persuasion, emotional connection, trust, impact on decision making, and contributing to positive organizational culture are without parallel—and no amount of data analytics can compete with them. (To be clear, we are not anti-data analytics; we just wanted to emphasize the point of how stories are more effective strategic tools if you want to get others to do something.)

How to Be a Good Storyteller

Nevertheless, even if you're not a Hollywood producer who traffics in stories day in and day out, it is possible for you to improve your own storytelling capabilities with a few research-based tips. After all, if you don't, you risk reduced engagement with stakeholders who may lose interest in what you're trying to accomplish, poorly communicate your vision, have trouble inspiring action; fail to connect emotionally; diminish your influence and persuasion, and handicap your ability to affect change and cultivate overall performance, among other things. All because you don't care about or invest in your own ability to tell stories.

Here's how you can become a better storyteller, just like our Hollywood producers:

1. **Remember that while your stories don't have to be long, they do need to have a beginning, middle, and an end.** When your stories have a clear structure, you activate the areas of the brain responsible for processing sequential information, which enhances understanding. And while this sequential information is being processed, it's best to limit them to no more than 2-3 minutes for maximum results.

2. **Employ vivid descriptions and sensory details.** Visual words like "clear," "bright," "crisp," and "dazzling" can help people see; Auditory words like "loud," "quiet," "whisper," "roar," and "silence" help people fear; Tactile words like "smooth," "rough," "soft," "slippery," and "velvety" help people get a sense of touch; Olfactory words like "sweet," "fresh," "musty," and sour help people get a sense of taste; and Emotional words like "joyful," "serene," "anxious," "excited," and "hopeful" can help people get a sense of emotion. The key here is not the specific word or words you use, but to include words that people can experience with their senses that are relevant to your story.

3. **Make sure your story is relevant.** By only using the most relevant information to inspire action toward a goal, you can avoid unnecessary detail that could distract or dilute the main message.

4. **Create characters and emotion arcs that people can connect with.** If, for example, your characters are facing a challenge and experiencing growth as a consequence, people will be rooting for them because you've triggered their mirror neurons and neurochemicals.

5. **Make sure to include surprising twists and turns.** When you throw in elements that people are not expecting, it stimulates curiosity and spurs on their attention. In other words, make sure you include items people do not see coming.

6. **Don't be afraid to use the "Pixar Storytelling Method."** The method is as follows: "Once upon a time there was [the ordinary world], every day [routine or situation], until one day [an inciting incident occurs], which leads to [a series of events and challenges], until finally [resolution and return to a new normal]". Of course, you don't have to

use the exact words "once upon a time," etc., but this gives you a formula you can follow to create compelling stories to capture your team's heart that captures all of the points listed above in a clear, succinct, and easy to understand way. And if it's worked for Pixar—to the tune of billions of dollars—it can work for you.

Ultimately, if you want to up your creative leadership game, invest in your storytelling capacities with these tips—just like Arthur and Allison did so many years ago when they first became producers. And speaking of Allison, you may be wondering what happened at the end of her story about the raving middle-aged man who was letting his kids do ecstasy that we promised to get to. This is what she told us,

"It's really interesting how it unfolded because the mom found out about it. And she ended up taking him to court. There was a point where he was around during this, so we were there to film it. His young kids, who were fine by the way, all ended up stopping doing ecstasy themselves and teamed up to do an intervention to help him. So it was quite a crazy ride and the man was able to get the help he needed."

CASE STUDY: ARTHUR SMITH'S MASTERCLASS IN STORYTELLING FOR LEADERS

Arthur Smith's success can be boiled down to this: his ability to tell a great story (not only on television, but in the boardroom, to his employees, to investors and studios, and to anybody he meets). And as the legendary visionary behind *American Ninja Warrior*, he used this hard won storytelling intelligence to navigate uncharted waters to transform a seemingly improbable concept he came across into a primetime sensation, hooking millions of viewers on the larger-than-life "heroes' journeys" the show emphasizes.

But Arthur's engagement with *American Ninja Warrior* didn't begin as a fully-baked story; it began, as all once-in-a-lifetime stories do, with a stroke of curiosity. "G4, which was owned by Comcast, had been carrying this little Japanese show dubbed into English," he told us. "The network wasn't doing very well, except this show was getting a little blip. They showed it to me, and I thought it was kind of interesting. The thing I was most interested in about it was who was running the course and that they were failing all the time. The fact that it was a dental hygienist and a plumber and they were all falling and failing and I was rooting for them and there was something in the celebration of the attempt that just got to me." And that's when the lightbulb went on for him.

Without Arthur seeing the opportunity to hook the viewer's attention with the everyday competitors' personal stories, *American Ninja Warrior* would likely never have grown from what it was to what it eventually became.

In other words, without emphasizing the compelling stories behind the competitors—and not just the competition itself—the original show would not have succeeded in persuading him to be interested in producing it at a higher level, and it would not have succeeded once he did produce it at the highest level possible (not only in ratings and revenues, but its cultural impact saw thousands of real-life obstacle courses similar to *American Ninja Warrior* popping up around the United States and take off because they were so inspired by it). Arthur told us, "I'm not in the business of making shows; I'm in the business of making hits. That's what we strive for. We don't strive to sell just another show. One of the things that I believe in is I don't believe in having a long list of shows. To have success, I believe in having a smaller list. I remember once going to my office and everybody was looking at me like I had two heads because I wrote on the board: 'Develop less. Pitch less. Sell more.' And everybody was like, what? What are you talking about? And I go 'Develop less. Pitch less. Sell more.' Well, repeating it didn't make it any clearer, but I just kept repeating it and saying it louder." This philosophy really highlights the essence of why stories matter, and especially the right stories, because they make you, your brand, and your projects stand out in a way that can capture minds, hearts, and imaginations. This may be one reason why Arthur's team did heed his message of 'Develop Less, Sell More' and was able to put on some of the biggest hits on the air like *Hell's Kitchen*.

He told us, "*Ninja* was a real challenge because there's no logical reason why an obstacle course show should be on NBC in prime time. If we would have pitched that show, we would have never sold it. *Ninja* was a challenge because we had to find a way to make it broad. We had to make it appeal to females and families. We had to find a way to make it a compelling story." And they did.

Arthur's success with *American Ninja Warrior* underscores the importance of storytelling in creative leadership. By connecting emotionally with the contestants' journeys and celebrating their efforts, he crafted a narrative that resonated deeply with viewers. This emotional engagement is at the heart of effective leadership, as it engenders a sense of shared purpose and motivates teams to strive for excellence.

Key Takeaways

1. **Storytelling as a Powerful Tool**: Stories are not merely entertainment; they serve as powerful tools for communication, inspiration, education, and motivation. Throughout history, from ancient times to modern leaders like Lincoln and Mandela, storytelling has been pivotal in shaping identity, values, and beliefs. Effective creative leaders understand that stories resonate deeply and are more impactful in conveying messages than facts or logic alone.

2. **Neuroscience of Storytelling**: There is a biological basis for why stories captivate us. They activate parts of the brain associated with empathy and emotional response. When we hear a compelling story, our brains mirror the emotions and experiences of the storyteller or characters, releasing neurochemicals that mimic those felt by the storyteller. This neural coupling makes stories more memorable, easier to understand, and more persuasive compared to straightforward data.

3. **Benefits in Creative Leadership**: Creative leaders who master storytelling benefit in multiple ways. They enhance engagement, emotional connection, and trust within their teams. Studies show that leaders who incorporate storytelling into their leadership style are perceived as more effective and can significantly improve organizational change initiatives. Storytelling helps leaders inspire action, create a positive organizational culture, and navigate complex ethi-

cal dilemmas by framing challenges in a relatable narrative format.

CHAPTER 6
IT'S NOT WHO YOU THINK THAT HOLDS THE SECRET TO YOUR FUTURE

"If you want to go fast, go alone. If you want to go far, go with others."[1]
— **African Proverb**

American Ninja Warrior Executive Producer Arthur Smith can perhaps be described as a jack-of-all-trades and master of many. Or, as people in Hollywood say, a successful producer.

Starting out as a college valedictorian, he quickly found his way as an actor, voice over artist, youngest-ever head of CBC Sports in Canada, programming head of FOX Sports, and head of a media empire turning out multiple long-running, hit network TV series thousands of miles away from his hometown of Montreal. But how did he get there?

Arthur tells us:

"I believe that you can't achieve your full potential [as a creative leader] unless you reach beyond what you think you can do. When you reach, you find out what you're capable of."

Interestingly, Arthur may be best known for developing "*Hell's Kitchen*." The long-running hit series was inspired by a U.K. show of the same name. But the similarities end there. Arthur's version completely reimagined food TV and was produced to appeal to a broad audience, regardless of whether they were foodies or not. With a brash host, high stakes, and authentic drama, the competition held the promise of a new culinary career for the winner. There had never been a successful network food show until then. As a result, *Hell's Kitchen* which is now going into its 23rd season spawned a whole entire sub-genre of television.

What Arthur illustrated to us is that, even if you're not all-in from the outset, even if you're unsure about something, it's okay to keep digging. To take a chance. To see where things might go. To experiment, like any creative leader would. To work on a project that's outside your normal area of focus, like food in this case. After all, once you find that star team-member, they can outperform an average one by over 400% and increase revenue by 67% across multiple industries according to studies (as Arthur proved when his show, *Hell's Kitchen*, became the longest running reality series on Fox and changed the landscape for how food is talked about in America) [2,3].

Collaborating With and Hiring The Right People

The ability to work with others, especially hiring or collaborating with those who are very different from you, is key. But the sad reality is that most hiring decisions in traditional organizations do not favor hiring the best or most qualified candidate, based on a Kellogg School of Management study [4]; they favor hiring the people who are just like the interviewers in how they think, talk, dress, and look. Ironically, it's no wonder that three out of every four organizations later admit to hiring the wrong people, costing the economy billions.

In other words, unlike taking an approach to working with somebody different from himself like Arthur, most companies are not hiring for diverse, complementary skills, personalities, and backgrounds. There are varied reasons for this—including the idea that there is only "one right way to hire" or "one right person to hire"—but one of the biggest is that traditional organizations rely on "gut" decisions using unstructured interview processes and assessments that later turn out to be wrong. They engage in what scholars call "the illusion of objectivity"—or the mistaken idea that we can be objective or fair, especially when we come across people who remind us of ourselves. [5] This is how it works in practice: If two job candidates have the same qualifications for the job but one went to your alma mater and just so happened to be in the same fraternity or sorority you were in—but the other didn't—you can easily guess who you will give the job to. The problem is, this phenomenon doesn't just exist with favoring alumni from our college or Greek house, it extends across a wide variety of other known or unknown preferences of interviewers and organizations that, taken together, handicap the hiring process.

One way a creative leader guards against this is to change how you write up job descriptions. For example, the average job description asks for a list of qualifications: years of experience doing a certain kind of job and an accompanying skill set. While this is logical, it doesn't work, as it is narrowing our ability to look for people who could be a great fit but who may not have a linear, traditional background that the job description arbitrarily articulates.[6] Here's what a creative leader like Arthur does instead,

"I believe that smart people can do anything. I'm really big on not typecasting people. From personal experience as a guy who was an actor, a producer, an executive and who now runs his own production company, I know that great people can adapt and succeed in all kinds of roles, regardless of their experience. I've had my mentors in life, like the legendary Dick Clark. I was a young sports producer from Canada. What business did I have producing award shows or game shows in America? Dick Clark saw something in me that made him trust me and my instincts. He knew that whatever I didn't know, I could learn on the fly."

What the creative leader does is they look for something traditional leaders do not: people who have the intellectual curiosity and flexibility to figure out how to get nearly anything done even if they've never done it before. In Robert and Michele Root-Bernstein's classic book, *Sparks of Genius: The 13 Thinking Tools of the World's Most Creative People*, they outline what many of the qualities a creative leader could look for when bringing new people onto a team: people who are very observational, questioning of the status quo, hands-on experimental types, synthesizers of broad knowledge, and able to generate essential principles or ideas from specific experiences or examples, among other things.[7]

Robert McNamara, the former CEO of Ford Motor Company turned Secretary of Defense turned head of the World Bank, was great at this; when asked how he could lead such diverse industries in the automobile, defense, and finance industries, he boiled down his thinking tools quite simply.[8] He responded that 90% of every leaders' job was the same: have a vision, set an audacious goal, figure out how to inspire the right people to work toward reaching the goal, and recalibrate when things aren't working. He said the other 10% was to learn the specific norms, practices, terminology, and content of whatever industry he was in. Put differently: other than this, all leadership is really the same stuff regardless of who or what you are leading.

Today, 94% of all job recruiters say the same thing. For example, they say "soft skills" like self-awareness, emotional intelligence, effective communication, curiosity, lifelong learning, and the like are much more important in potential hires than the "hard skills" that most job posts list.[9]

Harry Friedman, whom you met earlier, agrees:

"I've had the pleasure and pride of watching several people who had worked for me in entry level positions grow into capable, successful leaders. They each possessed some essential leadership traits, but perhaps what I appreciated most was their innate curiosity and desire to learn about all aspects of the business."

Creative Strategies For Hiring The Right People

So the question for you, as a growing creative leader, is how do you turn this great information about hiring smart, talented, curious people into a strategy you can use in your own work? After all, finding the right person is both difficult, as hundreds of applications come in for a single job (and 85% of job applicants admit to lying on their resume) and costly (employers spend between 50% to 200% of an employee's salary to replace a wrongly hired one) [10] [11].

If you have the time, check out the books *Who: A Method for Hiring* [12]; *The Best Team Wins: Building Your Teams Through Predictive Hiring* [13]; and *The Culture Code: Secrets of Highly Successful Teams*. They will allow you to dig more deeply into various hiring approaches [14]. But before we leave you with a few examples of innovative hiring policies we find valuable, we wanted to share an anecdote from Lloyd J. Schwartz about how he finds the "right fit" candidate that might be helpful for you. Lloyd told us,

"I'm really interested in the questions they ask of me to see if they've done their homework. I'm also interested in how they react to various things. For instance, when they leave I bring in the assistant and ask them, what were they really like in the waiting room? Because a lot of times, job candidates come in and put on an act in front of me. I want to know what they're acting like when they're not in front of me. I will also sometimes say something a little outrageous in the interview just to see how they react. To see whether they play along with it or not as a way to see who they really are."

In addition to the above, here are a few more untraditional creative strategies for trying to hire the right people beyond the standard "tell me about yourself/tell me about a time when" interview:

The first is **simulation-based hiring** of the Swiss giant IKEA . Instead of traditional interviews, candidates are invited to participate in hands-on activities ("job auditions") and role-playing exercises that simulate candidates problem-solving abilities, customer service skills, and compatibility with the company's values.[15]

The second is **personality-based hiring** that creative companies like Google, Microsoft, Goldman Sachs, Proctor and Gamble, and others use.[16-18] There are various tests out there like OCEAN, Myers-Briggs, and others to use to better assess not only the personality of a job candidate, but their potential strengths and weaknesses, the kinds of team members they might be, and the work environments they thrive in. [19, 20] You can also use these tests to see how they might fit on a team you're thinking about placing them in and where friction could arise based on their personality profile (as opposed to guessing because you couldn't see their drawbacks or a more accurate picture during a traditional interview). While this might seem like overkill, studies show that personality tests are an incredibly effective indicator of job performance (as are simulation-based role playing interviews).

Creatively choosing—and then investing in—the right collaborators and team as Arthur Smith and Harry Friedman have done will make all the difference as to whether you will move your ideas and projects forward to successful completion (and possibly achieve outsized success and results in the process). And you will need to do this better than ever before, as the competition has never been stiffer.

CASE STUDY: ALLISON GRODNER'S FORMULA: SECRETS TO FUTURE-PROOF LEADERSHIP

Allison Grodner, an Emmy® Award-winning producer known for her warm, creative leadership style, understands deeply the challenges of recruiting and hiring within the entertainment industry. The industry is, as will be discussed in the next chapter of the book, the most competitive in the world, and far more competitive than even institutions like Princeton, MIT, and the Navy Seals, so figuring out how to sort through the talent pool requires incredible finesse and hard work (something producers are constantly having to do).

For Allison, finding the right team members has always been akin to discovering hidden gems in The Grand Canyon. But she told us that it's even harder now, given the shift in expectations among many younger professionals: "It's been really interesting over the past few decades seeing the evolution of that young 20 something, and not necessarily always in a good way. It seems it's harder to find people who just want to come in and just be there and absorb and learn and do everything, and who aren't immediately concerned about, you know, when they'll get promoted or their titles." This shift, Allison observes, often manifests as a sense of entitlement, where the notion of "paying your dues" seems to have fallen by the wayside—but this paying of your dues, taking nothing for granted, and staying humble is what sets those destined to become creative leaders apart from everyone else. In fact, the most creative leaders are usually marked by their desire to want to do something—or try something or experiment with something—and not just be "somebody" so their egos can be stroked.

"It's really all about the journey and not the destination," Allison reflects. "Cliché, but I think that I was one of those overachievers, Type A personalities that a lot of us are. I read Orson Welles books and I was like, if I don't have that block-buster film by 19, I failed. But I think that it's really about jumping in and taking those risks and not worrying about get-ting those milestones that everyone and society tells you that you should get. This mindset will help you in terms of the unexpected curve balls that come your way and I wish more [young] people would embrace this. There is really no need to live on an artificial timeframe or try to achieve things by a certain age because you feel insecure, impatient, or want to impress people. All you need to do is focus on learning and growing and success will inevitably follow."

In Allison's eyes, the most valuable team members are those who embody a proactive spirit and a genuine appreciation for the creative journey. When hiring, she's looking not for those who fit the "traditional mold"—those only with Bachelors or Masters in Fine Arts or MBAs—but for those who possess enthusiasm, adaptability, and a willingness to learn. "I'm al-ways looking for someone who is proactive… for people who are curious, adaptable, and willing to take risks. It's not about finding someone who checks all the boxes but about finding someone who can bring something new to the table, who can grow with the project and the team."

Allison's emphasis on these qualities is a direct challenge to the traditional hiring practices that often favor candidates who fit a narrow set of criteria. Many organizations fall into the trap of hiring individuals who resemble their current staff, which limits diversity and innovation, and often works as an invisible trap undermining their growth. Allison told us, "When you do this for a while, you get stuck doing the same thing and you're like, oh, it's working. It's fine. You get a little lazy, you get a little comfortable. And I think that it's really important to keep evolving and to keep an open mind to the idea that there's some things that you still have yet to learn that you aren't necessarily doing completely right and there's maybe better ways to do it at times [and people you never considered before who can help you do it]."

One way having a unique team with a variety of backgrounds helped Allison was when COVID-19 threatened to halt the production of *Big Brother*. Together, Allison and her team used their diverse backgrounds and qualifications to craft a comprehensive 200-page document detailing COVID protocols—one of the first in the entertainment industry, if not the nation— ensuring the show could resume safely. "There was the question during COVID whether we would be producing *Big Brother*. But we wrote the whole book on how to get a show up and running with COVID protocols. We obviously pivoted to an all-star cast that season. And, we were one of the first shows of our size to start up again."

This proactive approach is a testament to Allison's belief in the power of teams that are flexible, creative, and enthusiastic and who can adapt to unforeseen challenges and create new solutions as a result. Interestingly, more diverse teams outperform non-diverse teams on nearly every measure according to studies, so Allison is onto something.

But this necessity for diversity in teams, especially in teams with gender balance, has not always been something Allison has historically observed Hollywood doing in its hiring and promoting practices. Allison told us, "While there are now many female executives and show runners, we are still battling double standards and stereotypes and assumptions brought on by gender norms and unconscious bias," which has often subjected her to personal attacks and unfounded assumptions about her career advancements simply because she is a woman.

In other words, Allison has seen her career challenged, the hiring of more women criticized (at one point in the recent past, less than 15% of Hollywood crew members were female), and resistance to creating diverse teams, even though she has outperformed her male counterparts time and time again.

But despite this, Allison finds satisfaction in mentoring other women and helping them overcome these barriers, especially in the mostly-male hiring process. "One of the most satisfying things about being a woman in this industry is when I am approached by other women and asked for career advice…so I share my story and lessons learned so that maybe they can be further ahead of where I was when I started so they can catapult to truly extraordinary outcomes." We couldn't have said it better ourselves.

Key Takeaways

1. **Embrace Collaboration and Risk-Taking:** Arthur Smith's career trajectory underscores the importance of reaching beyond one's comfort zone and collaborating with unlikely partners. His success with Gordon Ramsay on *Hell's Kitchen* demonstrates that even if initially skeptical, being open to new ideas and partnerships can lead to groundbreaking achievements.

2. **Challenge Legacy Hiring Practices:** Traditional organizations often fall into the trap of hiring individuals who resemble current staff in appearance and thinking, leading to missed opportunities and poor hires. Creative leaders should rethink job descriptions to focus on qualities like intellectual curiosity and adaptability rather than strictly adhering to a checklist of qualifications.

3. **Value Soft Skills in Hiring:** Soft skills such as curiosity, emotional intelligence, and effective communication are increasingly valued over hard skills by employers. These qualities enable individuals to adapt, learn, and lead effec-

tively across different industries and roles, as illustrated by Robert McNamara's career across automobile, defense, and finance sectors.

4. **Innovative Hiring Strategies:** Companies like IKEA and tech giants use innovative hiring methods such as simulation-based assessments and personality tests to identify candidates who not only fit the role but also contribute positively to team dynamics. These methods go beyond traditional interviews to predict job performance more accurately.

CHAPTER 7

THE ONLY COMPETITION
YOU CAN WIN

*"I have been up against tough competition all my life; I wouldn't
know how to get along without it."*
— **WALT DISNEY**

The most famous woman in the world was about to arrive
for a taping and *Black-ish* writer-producer Laura Gutin saw
her entire team freak out. In Hollywood, where everyone is
used to being the most recognized person in the room, watching studio execs, star actors, and crew members behave so un-
characteristically was ironic—and heartwarming.

Laura, who is an NAACP Image Award winner, told us,

"It was hilarious because everyone from the head of the
studio…to the entire wardrobe department, who rarely came
to set, showed up. They even had to get background checks
and security clearances…and it was all really crazy and really
fun. And it was just such a sense of accomplishment when it
was over."

The specific event in discussion was an episode Laura wrote
that Michelle Obama would be starring in and everyone wanted to be a part of it. While the reaction of these insiders might
not seem unusual in meeting the first African American First

Lady of the United States, it was; Hollywood personnel are insanely busy and not easily impressed given their familiarity with celebrities, so ooing and awwing over somebody is not something they normally do. And they don't normally do this because they are some of the most accomplished people alive who work in the most competitive industry in the world.

For example, Harvard accepts around 3% of its applicants and Google around 0.67% of its job seekers, but Hollywood only greenlights 0.01% of all television shows and movies pitched. [1][2][3] And it accepts only an infinitesimally small number of people who audition for acting roles or behind-the-scenes crew gigs. In other words, even the most competitive universities and private companies are not nearly as competitive as the entertainment business, so Laura believes Hollywood has a lot of insight for industries of all sorts when it comes to competition. We agree.

But every other aspect of entertainment—the streaming wars, Box office numbers, film festivals, awards races like the Oscars® and Emmys®—these phenomena are all likewise very competitive. And that's a good thing. Competition accounts for up to 30% of productivity growth in the United States and has led to many of the luxuries we enjoy today, not just in entertainment but also in technology and countless daily amenities.[4]

Allison Grodner, whom you met earlier in the book, told us,

"We're in a competitive environment…and it's hard. I'm not going to lie or sugar coat it…it's just the nature of the business. But I'm also blessed to be in the position that I'm in to have a good reputation and have some key shows on the air that have given me more opportunities."

Allison is blessed, as is Laura, not only because they have found massive success, but because they have mastered the **3 types of competition** creative leaders need to thrive in nearly every industry. These types of competition must be continuously mastered and re-mastered.

First Type of Competition: Competing With Yourself

For creative leaders like Allison and Laura, all competition starts with themselves. That is, they look at the first aspect of competition as setting personal development goals, not necessarily beating others. Yes, they want to win, but stretching themselves beyond their current boundaries is a major intrinsic motivator, the strongest type of motivator there is. In fact, across all industries, 80% of employees feel more motivated to improve their performance when they set personal goals that challenge them beyond their current capabilities—and perhaps goals that even scare them a bit.

Laura said,

"It's about doing it for yourself…and looking back 25 years later, I'm very proud of this circuitous route I've taken in this career because it's not a straight line. It's not just continuing to climb a ladder. There were rungs that were missing. There were times I slipped back down. And so I'm really proud I've been able to put together a career in the entertainment business because it is just very hard to work in. And even if you "make it" that doesn't mean it's permanent. I love what it took to get me here and to keep getting ready. When I had two kids, for example, I thought they were going to kick me off of the carousel in favor of someone who could be more flexible, and I wasn't sure if I would ever be allowed back on. I did successfully get back on and I'm more proud of that than anything else."

In other words Laura demonstrated the idea that, as the great 7-time Super Bowl Champion Tom Brady said, "I didn't come this far only to come this far." [5] She views her career as an ever-evolving journey with new goals and milestones to be achieved, new lessons to be learned, and a new creative leader to be developed within herself. And how did Laura do this specifically? She set SMART goals –Specific, Measurable, Achievable, Relevant, and Time-bound goals [6]; kept a Progress Journal (to track accomplishments, setbacks, and patterns of professional behavior) [7] ; conducted regular Self-Assessments (to determine areas to improve in) [8]; and invested in Continuous Learning (courses, workshops, and seminars) time and time again to successfully compete with herself [9].

Second Type of Competition: Competing Against Your Team

Although many people find it off putting, another approach many creative leaders engage in to refine expertise and skills is encouraging their team members to compete against, not just with, their team. For example, organizations that encourage this type of healthy (and not toxic version of) internal competition are 140% more likely to have a culture of innovation according to PriceWaterhouseCoopers [10]. They are also more likely to outperform teams who don't compete internally by 30%, experience less employee turnover, and have more than 80% of their employees feel engaged and satisfied at work. [11],[12] Of course, there is a toxic version of this too: credit grabbing, hoarding information, micromanaging, sabotage, and excessive stress that you will want to avoid.

Allison, who has won multiple Emmys®, saw healthy internal competition first hand by compassionately encouraging her employees to compete with each other—which resulted in sky-high ratings, financial abundance, and critical success. More to the point, Allison was able to refine her team's expertise and skills in a proactive way by not only providing psychological safety, but also clearly defining goals and metrics for them. Everyone was evaluated so that they would have an equal shot at success. She publicly celebrated team members' individual performance when it was merited, applauding individuals and encouraging other team members to go after higher performance themselves. She offered timely rewards and incentives. Most importantly, she helped her employees set personal goals that were linked with the team's, which Gallup surveys show overwhelmingly contributes to a successful workplace environment.

However, Allison also saw the other side of this equation when these same high-performing employees, whom she groomed for years to one day be creative leaders of their own, eventually left to start their own successful companies. She told us,

"It's bittersweet. But I'm also happy because they're people who have worked for me. And so it's really hard to get upset because it's nice to see people own their own companies, run their own shows, and sell their own ideas. It's great to see and it's nice to think that maybe I helped play a small part in that."

This, perhaps more than anything else, is a testament to Allison's greatness. Not only was she able to see that her training and development of her team helped them find success for her projects, but her training and development helped them find success for their own projects. And it makes perfect sense: once you teach people how to fly, many of them will one day want to independently soar—and that's perfectly okay.

Third Type of Competition: Competing With Emotion

The third type of competition a creative leader faces is the least familiar: competing with emotion. But what Laura revealed about this, through relaying an anecdote about working with Michelle Obama, speaks eye-opening volumes,

"Observing Mrs. Obama was very interesting because I had never thought about the amount of other people's feelings you hold when you're in that [leadership] position…I mean, you had all of these people lining up to tell her their story and what she meant to them. And I think that's a lot of psychic energy to hold for one person…and it just gave me a real appreciation for all of the parts of people's jobs that we don't see."

For any leader, but especially for creative leaders, the emotions of the entire organization—of direct reports, teams, and people who never interact with the boss—are often overlooked. Part of the reason for this is because for decades America so heavily bought into the behaviorism of the American psychologist B.F. Skinner who rejected emotions as being unimportant.[13] Another reason for this is because, according to studies, traditional leaders' brains become neurochemically less able to comprehend others' emotions the higher they climb. [14] But understanding emotion, even more than having razor-sharp logical reasoning skills, is what differentiates the creative leader from the traditional one, both biologically and in practice).

In other words, one of the primary distinctions of the creative leader is an empathy-based approach. And empathy can be thought of in three parts: cognitive empathy (or understanding other people's perspectives); emotional empathy (feeling what other people are feeling); and responsive empathy (knowing how to compassionately respond to other people's emotions). [15]

Put differently, this EQ is extremely important to master as leaders who promote emotional wellness—companies like Salesforce and LinkedIn—outperform those that don't.[16] Why? Because they foster better workplace engagement, teamwork, and customer relationships, among other things, which are the real drivers of motivation and success. As it turns out, using mere logical strategy, systems, and strategic planning can cause many employees of traditionally led firms to underperform. Just as there is little human touch, so too is there little incentive to go all out for the more emotionally indifferent, cold, or hostile organizations.[17]

Of course, there are examples of "creative leaders" who don't have EQ, but they are rare beyond anecdotal data.

So what Allison and Laura have shown here is that, when it comes to the three types of competition—competing with yourself, against your team, and with emotions—requires constantly refining your expertise and skills. Without this refinement, and without curiosity, becoming a creative leader will be difficult to impossible. But with these things, you can accelerate your own leadership, which you will need to do especially when making difficult decisions, the subject of our next chapter.

CASE STUDY: LAURA GITLIN'S STRATEGY: CONQUERING THE THREE TYPES OF COMPETITION

In Hollywood, where competition is fierce and the stakes are high, creative leaders must navigate challenges that test their resolve, ingenuity, and emotional intelligence. For Laura Gutin, a writer-producer known for her work on *Black-ish*, competition isn't just a part of the industry; it's an essential element that either makes or breaks you given the gladiatorial-like way the freelance entertainment business is structured. Laura told us,

"I came out to Los Angeles and I got my first job and thought, Okay, now I work in Hollywood. And then the show ended and I had to find another job and start all over. And then that job ended and I had to find another job. That's when it finally sank in that I was going to have to start over and over and over again. You know, so many people who end up in Hollywood are these high achievers who did really well in school and got congratulated for that and rewarded for that. And then all of a sudden, you're in an industry where you can work really hard, you can get every answer correct on the test, and you still fail. And I think you learn to find the strength inside yourself instead of seeking validation from others. Because you can do something that you feel really good about, and nobody notices. And you could do something that feels like a throwaway, and people will love it, and you feel a little bit like, oh, that piece of garbage. And so I think you have to stop waiting for other people's approval, and just ask yourself, 'Am I happy? Do I feel like I'm doing work that I'm proud of? Do I feel like I'm doing things every day that are gonna get me where I want to be?'"

"You know *Blackish* was such a huge success. And it was a really wonderful place to work and all that. But I had great experiences on other shows that were total bombs. But people don't remember those because I spent so much time at *Black-ish*. I was on shows that lasted only one season before they were canceled or where we only did 13 episodes. But I learned so much, I grew as a writer, and I made friendships. And you know, these professional friendships and personal friendships are what have sustained me. And so again, you know, sometimes you tell people, 'I worked on this show' and they say dismissively, 'Oh, that thing.' And I get why they say that, I get that that is their outside perspective. But from my inside perspective, that show they 'dissed' was the best show I ever worked on and helped me grow more than they could ever know."

What Laura is getting at here is that creative leaders have to create different measurements of success than they used to have in order to become fulfilled in their work and keep pushing forward in their careers. Because there are not only massive amounts of uncertainty in business, but wildly different reactions people will have about what you're doing and you will have to define what success looks like and what it doesn't—and not just take others' metrics or society's metrics or judgments or reactions as your own. This is the first rule of competition; without it, you will crumble under the weight of pressure, expectations, and the often arbitrary nature of social and business approval and disapproval. With it, you will thrive. "You just have to learn to calm down and let things happen and just follow your path wherever it goes, because I think if you rigidly try to stay on a path you've constructed in your mind, you will blow up," Laura continued. "Have you just hit a dead end and do you know how to get over it? If you haven't built up the resiliency and those skills to look at an obstacle and go, 'Okay, how do I get past this?' you are setting yourself up for a fall. Instead of thinking, "Oh, I've worked hard, and I now that I've gotten here, this boulder shouldn't be here, you should be thinking with every new mountain I climb I'm going to be facing boulders I never envisioned, never planned or prepared for, or never was told about—and that's ok."

Laura also told us a second rule when it comes to competition that many leaders often fail to realize before it's too late. "Comparison is the death of creativity and, I think, it is also the death of careers. And the people that I know, from when I was starting out, and over the years who spent the most time saying, 'why do they have what I don't have?' are the people who would always say to me, 'how did you get that job?' They don't last very long or rise very high—or if they do somehow, they often fail spectacularly or make everyone around them miserable— because of their jealousy and comparison."

For Laura, healthy competition starts from within and it doesn't really think about what others are doing. It simply sets its path and sees how to make the best out of what life and circumstances throw its way. Laura concluded by quoting the show *30 Rock*, which we received well as a great lesson for all of us, "have some self-respect, don't you know you can fly?"

Key Takeaways

1. **Creative Competition Drives Achievement:** The story of Laura Gutin and Michelle Obama's appearance on Black-ish illustrates how creative competition can inspire teams to excel. Despite Hollywood's competitive nature, the anticipation and preparation for a significant event like this not only brought excitement but also a sense of accomplishment among the team members.

2. **There are Different Levels of Competition Across Industries**: Hollywood exemplifies an exceptionally competitive environment, with only 0.1% of television shows and movies making it past the pitching stage. This level of competition, akin to or exceeding that of prestigious

universities and top corporations, underscores the valuable insights that creative industries can offer to other sectors.

3. **Competing With Yourself:** Successful creative leaders, such as Laura Gutin and Allison Grodner, emphasize personal development as a cornerstone of competition. They set ambitious personal goals, continually push boundaries, and view setbacks as part of a circuitous and invaluable career journey rather than meaningless obstacles.

4. **Internal Team Competition:** Encouraging healthy competition within teams can foster innovation and excellence. Allison Grodner's approach of fostering internal competition among her team members not only propelled performance but also created a supportive environment where both individual and collective achievements were celebrated, and individuals were motivated to excel.

5. **Competing with Emotion:** The concept of competing with emotion highlights the importance of empathy and emotional intelligence (EQ) in creative leadership. Understanding and responding to the emotions of team members and stakeholders can significantly enhance team cohesion, engagement, and ultimately, organizational success.

CHAPTER 8

CHEAT CODES FOR MAKING DIFFICULT DECISIONS

"The key to making good decisions is not knowledge. It is understanding. We are swimming in the former. We are desperately lacking in the latter." [1]
— **Malcolm Gladwell**

Producer Fanshen Cox, a childhood best friend of Ben Affleck and Matt Damon, was facing one of the most difficult decisions of her career: whether she should try to convince Ben and Matt to make a pet project she fell in love with or put it on the shelf because there were just so many unknown variables and risks.

Fanshen told us,

"I think the hardest decision I had to make was letting go of a Sci Fi fantasy project I pitched to Matt and Ben. It was in a genre I knew nothing about and was only pitching because I was in love with one aspect of it, and not the many other aspects it needed to have to be successful...I had to check my humility, which is really hard to do sometimes."

Academy Award winning producer Andrew Carlberg, who has also received an Emmy®, agrees,

"We need to know when not to make a movie. We need to know when the universe is telling us we shouldn't be making it because we don't have the right actors attached, we don't have the financing, and that it would be irresponsible for us to do this."

Time and time again, Fanshen and Andrew mentioned how much restraint they had to exercise in making decisions, one of the keys to their incredible success.

In other words, Fanshen and Andrew have had to consistently demonstrate the kind of humility creative leaders need because it is easy to become blinded by overconfidence (especially when one is successful). After all, in a Duke Study of business executives, this is one of the greatest goliaths for leaders: overconfidence.[2] A full 80% of leaders are overconfident in their judgment and abilities according to the statistics. [3]

Other studies confirm the same reality: Research by Harvard Business Review has found that even good leaders frequently make very bad decisions.[4]

Why Is It So Hard For Leaders To Make Good Decisions?

Before diving into the difference in the decision making process between the creative leader and the traditional one, it's important to note that there are many things that could cause decisions to go south: overconfidence is one, personality conflicts and political contests are others, and how they think is perhaps the most dangerous of all.

In perhaps one of the most groundbreaking and influential studies in the field of decision science, for example, economist Daniel Kahneman and colleagues observed in the 1970s that leaders use heuristics (or mental shortcuts) often to their detriment when deciding on things both big and small.[5] In other words, what leaders see as 'conventional wisdom,' how they (often wrongly) interpret the efficacy of their own experience, and their underestimation of their own shortcomings, blinds them. In particular, what Kahneman found about every decision-making leader, especially if they are a creative leader dealing with increasing uncertainty, was the following:

Confirmation bias: the tendency to seek information that confirms their preexisting preferences, ignoring contradictory evidence [6];

Anchoring effect: allowing the first piece of information (the "anchor") presented to overly shape subsequent judgments and decisions [7];

Framing effect: similar to anchoring effect, how the same piece of information is presented (or "framed") from different angles can lead to different judgments and decisions [8];

Loss aversion: the preference for avoiding losses rather than going after gains [9];

Risk aversion: overly preferring to avoid risks, even when potential unknown gains outweigh potential known gains [10];

Decision fatigue: making too many decisions under stress, resulting in mental resources being depleted and poor-quality decisions. [11]

These blind spots, which influence 8 out of every 10 decisions, are a huge reason why many leaders think they're making high quality decisions when, most of the time, they are not, according to data.[12] The leader thinks they have the one "right decision," but they do not. And regardless of what type of leader they are—for example, regardless of whether they are a visionary, democratic, autocratic, transformational, servant, charismatic, or laissez-faire leader—every leadership style is prone to these blind spots (with different blind spots influencing different types of leaders). In addition, creative leaders can be mindful of how groupthink and pluralistic ignorance can hijack their team's overall ability to make sound decisions. Groupthink reflects a psychological phenomenon where the desire for harmony and conformity in a group leads to irrational or dysfunctional decision-making. Pluralistic ignorance, on the other hand, occurs when members of a group mistakenly believe that their own thoughts or feelings are different from others, leading them to conform to the perceived views of the group. Thus, it behooves creative leaders to effectively steer away from these troublesome dynamics.

For example, in 2001, Segway's leaders didn't examine their confirmation biases (or customer's loss aversions) and convinced one another that their decision to launch a Segway product would create a huge consumer demand for customers to get rid of their own bicycles. It was a spectacular failure.[13] Likewise, in the early 2010s, Yahoo! Inc's shareholders underestimated the decision fatigue of their company because of constant leader turnover and endless decisions they had to make about changes in products, services, and strategies as a result, leading to huge losses for the organization.[14]

On the other hand, in 2017, the leaders of Nintendo, Inc. rightly understood their own risk aversion biases (to keep designing traditional home based game consoles because that was their profit center) but threw it out of the window once they realized they could introduce their revolutionary portable Switch game console and appeal to a new gamer they hadn't traditionally targeted. Without alienating their traditional home-gaming customer, they were convinced they could send sales through the roof with the portable console gamer.[15] The same is true for IBM in the early 1990s.[16] They too had risk aversion like Nintendo—in their case, it was switching away from hardware as their focus—but they realized that investing in "software as a service" (or Saas) would be their future because software adoption avoided the loss aversion for customers who had already purchased hardware.

Arthur Smith, whom you met earlier, shared an experience about a decision he had to make when he was running coverage for the Olympics that overcame some of these entrenched biases from his organization's various leaders. In particular, he told us about a high-pressure time when he had to make a decision that many of his colleagues disagreed with, perhaps because of confirmation biases and risk aversion as detailed above. Arthur said,

"I was producing the Seoul Olympic Games for CBC in Canada and they were calling the event 'The Race of the Century' between Canadian sprinter Ben Johnson and defending Olympic gold medalist Carl Lewis. It was an incredible race. Ben won the Gold and set a world record in the process. Our broadcast set the record for the highest rated program in the history of Canadian television…Three days later I was awoken in the middle of the night because Ben had tested positive for performance enhancing drugs. I sent multiple camera crews all over the city to cover the story in depth from every possible angle and woke up my lead anchor in the middle of the night to go on the air…I made the decision to stop covering the Games for over 90 commercial-free minutes because I felt that this story was bigger than the Olympics itself. A number of the producers who were working for me insisted I was making a mistake by solely focusing on this story and not covering the Olympics. There was a hotline phone between me in Seoul and the head of the network in Toronto that rarely rang. When it did, I was expecting to get chewed out for not covering the Olympics, but instead the network boss assured me that the entire country was watching and that I had made the right decision. That choice, to follow my instincts, resulted in the highest rated night in Canadian television history, with more people in Canada seeing Ben Johnson's medal taken away than saw him win it in the first place. And if that wasn't enough, not only did our Olympic coverage win the Gemini Award (Canada's Emmy®) for best sports coverage of the year, the night that

Ben lost the medal was awarded the Gemini for best NEWS coverage of the year.

What Arthur did in this case was what great creative leaders like him do: they don't just use past data to inform current decisions. He eschewed the confirmation bias and risk aversion in the industry that assumed past analytics should make every decision . In this case, the prior analytics said to never cut away from a live sporting event as highly rated as the Olympics because it would sink viewership and commercial revenue. But instead of making old analytics his gospel, Arthur showed them that, while helpful and important a lot of the time, *they should not make heuristical decisions every time*, especially about new phenomena they have never measured or encountered before.

Personality Conflicts and Political Contests in Decision Making:

Another area that hijacks making good decisions is personality conflicts and internal politics. For example, many traditional leaders allow the decision-making process to be a battle of personal wills between people on their teams or in organizations rather than a collaborative process for arriving at the best possible ideas and solutions. Soon enough, people get offended, feelings get hurt, and personality conflict ruffles everyone's feathers, resulting in decisions that are bound to fail by the time resentful team members (who lost the personality or political contest) are asked to implement them.

Jonathan Murray, who in addition to creating *The Real World* was also producer of the longstanding hit show *Making The Band* alongside Sean "Puff Daddy"/"P Diddy"/"Diddy" Combs, vulnerably said that he couldn't work on the show with Combs because the decision making process became too fraught with personality issues and politics just like in any non-entertainment organization,

"I think it was one of the hardest decisions to make to walk away from *Making The Band*...MTV partnered us with Sean "Puffy" Combs [and] we did a successful season with him, but he was a challenge to work with...And so we we felt we were in the untenable position where we really couldn't produce the show...so we decided to walk away from it. Ultimately the show did 6 or 7 more [highly profitable] seasons, so it was a very expensive decision."

Let that sink in: Jonathan, as one of the most successful producers in Hollywood history, decided to leave a show he personally created because of personality conflicts—a decision that cost him millions of dollars. A GoodHire Survey also found that 82% of all employees across various industries leave organizations because of similar personality conflicts and political battles that traditional leaders have never reigned in because they assume "it is what it is."

A New Approach to Making Workplace Decisions: D.E.C.I.D.E.

But personality conflicts, political contests, and psychological blind spots can be overcome. Despite the fact that many leaders get bogged down in self-serving interpretations of information, informational jams that prevent data from being released, narrow perspectives, and occasional extortionists hijacking decision making, the decision making process can be smoother and, in fact, a successful, step-by-step process.

Before we share our process with you, which we call D.E.C.I.D.E., let us first briefly share the inherent differences in the decision making process between traditional leaders and creative ones.

On the one hand, traditional leaders often rely on: data-driven approaches that are analytical and predictable; hierarchical decision-making with limited input from multiple stakeholders; short-term foci and results; risk-aversion methodologies;

and status quo maintenance mechanisms. As we've seen, this usually results in poor decisions despite it seeming like the most logical thing to do.

On the other hand, creative leaders usually do the reverse. They mix data analysis from their industry or firm with proven ideas and data from other diverse industries, as well as their own intuition in a minority of cases. They involve many others for idea generation and feedback, regardless of how high or low they are in the organizational hierarchy. They center a long-term focus on vision with eventual and delayed results, and they target experimentation with new approaches. As studies also show us, these techniques yield much higher quality decisions and results in terms of productivity and performance, innovation, revenue growth, market success, and cost savings for firms led by these creative leaders.

So the results are in: to be a better creative leader, and to make better decisions like them, you can use the following creative model:

D.E.C.I.D.E.

- **D**efine–Clarify the decision to be made

- **E**valuate—Assess objective criteria for the decision

- **C**onsult—Gather input from many different types of stakeholders

- **I**dentify—Make the decision, preferably by getting buy-in but not consensus, from everyone

- **D**eploy—Implement the decision

- **E**xamine—Review and learn from the decision, do after-action reviews, and never use the "B" ("Blame") or "F" ("Fault") words if things didn't turn out the way you want them to

Netflix employed an approach like D.E.C.I.D.E. in the early 2000s when they pivoted from a DVD rental service to a streaming one, in which success was not a guaranteed result [17]. Ford used a model like this in 2018 when they ceased production on making sedans, marking a significant strategy shift to focus on their larger vehicle fleet like trucks and SUVS [18]. Apple followed a strategy like this in 2014 when they bought an outside company, Beats Electronics, an unusual move for the company as it primarily focused on making its own products and technology [19] Additionally, Tesla followed this type of model in 2014 when they open-sourced all of their electric vehicle patents to accelerate the adoption of electric vehicles by allowing competitors to copy their ideas and then invest their own billions of dollars to co-create a clean-energy infrastructure alongside them. [20]

Andrew helps put this perspective into even simpler terms,

"As [legendary director] Ron Howard once said, 'the best idea wins.'" And the best ideas are bound to win when they are tethered to a proven decision-making approach like D.E.C.I.D.E., not psychological biases, personality conflicts, or internal political battles. This is especially true when a creative leader needs to turn disaster into opportunity, where we head in the next chapter.

CASE STUDY: FANSHEN COX'S GUIDE TO HIGH STAKES DECISION-MAKING

Fanshen Cox sat in her cozy Los Angeles office, her mind whirling with thoughts and emotions. The decision she faced was monumental, a potential turning point in her career as a producer when a dream Sci-Fi project was pitched to her that she fell in love with. She had always been known for her keen eye for projects and her ability to bring stories to life, but this time was different. The stakes were higher given her personal connection to the material—she is married to a Trekkie (aka a huge Star Trek fan) and had a growing love of Sci-Fi—and because she prided herself on giving underrepresented writers whose voices are normally excluded in Hollywood a shot at pitching and proving themselves.

Despite this, the variables were more uncertain than ever before. She told us, "You know, the first thing that I always go back to is to check in with myself and my principles and values, and ask if a project aligns with my principles and values or not. And I have to search for humility and check my heart and see if I'm just putting my name on something or doing something that I think is gonna look good or because I have personal biases. And I have to search to see if I'm really just doing it out of emotion and not really thinking through every aspect of it."

This time the project under consideration was one she was deeply passionate about—a Sci-Fi fantasy epic written by a black writer. It was a genre she knew little about, yet there was something about the story that captivated her. The intricate world-building, the rich characters, and the profound themes all drew her in (think urban *Lord of the Rings*). However, despite her enthusiasm, she couldn't shake the nagging doubts in the back of her mind. The risks were enormous given the complexity of the technology, huge potential price tag, and reality that everything had to be filmed perfectly just to succeed.

Reflecting on her dilemma, Fanshen thought about her childhood friends from Boston, Ben Affleck and Matt Damon. They had always been her pillars of support, from their early days dreaming of Hollywood to their current status as industry icons. Convincing them to take on this project was tempting, but the responsibility weighed heavily on her shoulders.

She said, "We're all human, and we make mistakes. And you know, mistakes are an incredibly important part of the creative process. You can't get to where you want to get to without making them. But you want to make honest mistakes, not reckless ones because you refused to look at the facts and weigh whether the rewards were worth the risks."

Fanshen knew she had to exercise restraint. Her success had been built on making calculated decisions, not impulsive ones. Yet, the allure of an epic Sci-Fi project by a black writer was hard to ignore. She found herself caught between her principles and her pragmatic instincts.

She understood that seeking information that confirmed her preexisting preferences and allowing initial impressions to overly influence her judgments could lead her astray. She needed a clearer, more objective perspective. So she began by defining her decision. Was the Sci-Fi project truly the right move for her career and for Matt and Ben? Once she asked that question, she evaluated the objective criteria, considering the project's potential for success, the resources required, and the risks involved.

One evening, as the sun set over the Hollywood Hills, Fanshen found herself in communication with Ben and Matt, discussing the project. The conversation was heartfelt and honest. She laid out her passion for the story but also her concerns about the unknowns. Together, they weighed the pros and cons, considering both the artistic and practical aspects. "I had to go back to checking my principles and my values."

In the end, they decided to put the project on the shelf even though they loved everything about it artistically and creatively. It was a tough call, but the right one. Fanshen realized that true leadership often involves making difficult choices and recognizing when to step back; of balancing passion and pragmatism; and of knowing when to let go even when you really want to hang on.

Key Takeaways

1. **Humility and Restraint in Decision-Making**: Both Fanshen Cox and Andrew Carlberg emphasize the importance of humility when making decisions, especially in the entertainment industry. Fanshen reflects on the challenge of letting go of a project she loved but realized wasn't feasible, highlighting the need to check personal biases and acknowledge limitations.

2. **Overcoming Overconfidence**: Creative leaders often face the pitfall of overconfidence, which can lead to poor decision-making. Studies show that a majority of decisions made by traditional leaders are ineffective due to overconfidence in their judgments and abilities. This overconfidence blinds leaders to alternative perspectives and risks.

3. **Psychological Blind Spots**: Decision-making is influenced by psychological blind spots such as confirmation bias, anchoring effect, and loss aversion. These biases encourage leaders to favor information that confirms their preexisting beliefs, ignore contradictory evidence, and overly prefer avoiding risks, even when potential gains outweigh the losses.

4. **Impact of Personality Conflicts and Politics**: Personality conflicts and internal politics can significantly hinder decision-making processes. Jonathan Murray's decision to walk away from "Making The Band" due to conflicts with Sean Combs illustrates how personal dynamics can escalate and disrupt even successful projects, leading to costly decisions.

5. **D.E.C.I.D.E. Model**: The D.E.C.I.D.E. model (Define, Evaluate, Consult, Identify, Deploy, Examine) offers a structured approach to decision-making that contrasts with traditional hierarchical methods. It emphasizes gathering diverse inputs, considering long-term vision, and learning from outcomes through after-action reviews, rather than assigning blame.

CHAPTER 9

BEYOND THE FIRE: DANCING IN THE MAZE OF CRISIS MANAGEMENT

"The gem cannot be polished without friction, nor man perfected without trials." [1]
— **Chinese Proverb**

The clouds looked ominous, the sky appeared gray, and Harry Friedman had a knot in the pit of his stomach.

"My biggest challenges as a producer have had more to do with the welfare of the staff and crew than they did with the program itself, and called for leadership on an entirely different level."

Harry told us that, in addition to his run producing *Jeopardy!*, he had been producer of *Wheel of Fortune* when one of the most defining moments of his life happened. But why would such a fun show be so life-altering and leave him with a feeling of unease?

Harry continued,

"Wheel Of Fortune had established a tradition of taking the show on the road, producing up to 45 of each season's 195 episodes in different locations. These were ambitious and expensive remotes… we did more than 55 of them during my tenure …and in August 2005 we were taping at the New Orleans Convention Center. The plan was to tape 15 episodes, 5 a day on August 26th, 27th, and 28th. Around August 23rd we started hearing that Hurricane Katrina, which had just become a Category 5 in The Gulf of Mexico, was heading straight for New Orleans."

But hurricanes this large frequently diminish while they are still at sea, so was there anything to worry about? After all, of the around 80 tropical storms and hurricanes the world experiences annually, only a tiny percentage are Category 5s and ever make landfall.

"The locals kept reassuring us that this happens all the time; the weather forecasters throw everyone into a panic over a potential disaster that doesn't materialize because at the last minute, the hurricane changes course and the crisis is averted." And if we canceled a taping based on another false alarm, it would mean that every local crew member would unnecessarily lose out on a precious pay day.

But the National Weather Service forecasters were adamant that this time was different, and the management at our local TV station concurred. They began the painful process of notifying thousands of ticket holders that the third tape day was canceled.

We began the second day of taping knowing that at its completion, around 9:00 pm, we would start packing up in preparation for getting out of town the next day. What we couldn't have known was that while were shooting those last 5 shows, all of the flights into and out of the airport got canceled; all train travel had been halted; car rental agencies stopped answering their phone; and Harry's 75 crew members, who were moms and dads and sisters and brothers with families that deeply loved them, were in the bullseye of what would become one of the most devastating disasters in American history."

So Harry decided to act, to slip into crisis-management mode for the people whose lives he felt responsible for protecting. He said…

"I remembered that our hotel had buses for a couple of tour groups that were canceled…and after much wrangling we convinced them to relinquish their tour buses to us…[so] we boarded the buses and set out for Houston…In the first hour, on roads clogged with thousands of other vehicles, we traveled a total of 2 miles…And after 20 straight hours on the road, we [finally] made it to Houston and flew home. Once we got there, I turned on CNN and watched live coverage of the disaster we left behind, including images of the hall we occupied to film at the New Orleans Convention Center now submerged under 20 feet of water."

Had it not been for Harry's quick thinking—to get tour buses that he spotted out of the corner of his eye days before filming—he, and his crew, would not be here. In this moment, despite all of the success he has received before and since, he knew he was operating at his finest, using quick thinking—adaptive thinking, really—to make a life-saving decision for dozens of people and manage the crisis of his life.

Part of what made Harry so effective in managing this budding crisis was his ability to use divergent thinking—which explores and generates multiple possible solutions or ideas in often a nonlinear fashion in response to a problem (instead of focusing on finding a single, correct solution that many traditional leaders rely on).

Because he worked in the entertainment business as a producer, where job #1 is to be a creative "problem solver," he looked at this event as an opportunity to come up with different ideas and solve another problem—albeit an existential one. This positive mindset, of believing he could figure out a solution with his divergent thinking because he had done it many times before, also helped him regulate his cortisol (the body's stress chemical that gets released any time we are operating under pressure). As a consequence, it helped him stop the dangerous effects cortisol could have had on his performance. As an aside, cortisol during a crisis, or even just a stressful moment, results in: 1. Impaired decision making, impaired problem-solving, and impaired impulse control [2]; 2. Weakened immune systems, not only in increased heart rates, raised blood pressure, and sleep interference, but making us more at risk for major illnesses in real-time [3]; and 3. Diminished empathy, empathetic, which makes us less sensitive to others, and unable to manage communication, resulting in unnecessary misunderstanding and conflict.[4]

In other words, because Harry was comfortable using divergent thinking to problem solve as a producer, he was able to bypass his body's cortisol performance inhibitors and think quickly on his feet. And this is incredibly important for all creative leaders to do because the average organization experiences 3 crises in 5 years according to PriceWaterhouseCooper, so managing crises is one of the top requirements of a leader.[5] If a leader doesn't manage a crisis effectively, their company could lose millions of dollars. Unfortunately, 70% of companies have admitted that their leaders do not have the skill set or plan to avert disaster when it inevitably comes.[6]

Of course, not every crisis will be life threatening like the one Harry faced (though, interestingly, nearly every producer we interviewed for this book, including Mexican American producer Javier Chapa who has had several #1 Netflix and Amazon hits, told us that managing the complex healthcare and filming around the Covid-19 pandemic was one of the hardest things they've ever had to do.) Many crises are in fact logistical in nature, impact business operations, or can negatively affect reputation, which can produce just as much stress for our bodies as existential ones do, and which require divergent thinking just the same.

Hell's Kitchen producer Arthur Smith, for example, told us about the first time he was trying to produce a show called *I Survived a Japanese Game Show* in Tokyo. He said,

"The problem with shooting a show in Japan is studios are very hard to book, especially on short notice. There's also no house big enough to hold 16 people and all the cameras and other equipment. Things tend to move a little slower and are easily lost in translation. While we were going through the arduous process of locking down the logistics in Japan, the Executive Producer and Challenge Producer decided to quit the show because it seemed impossible that we would ever be able to pull it off. But we were steadfast in our determination to make it happen. Within a month we resolved ALL of the issues, including finding a house and fortunately, a cancellation at a studio gave us the last critical piece we needed to go to Japan and make this one of a kind show. The show was not only a ratings hit on ABC, but was the winner of the Rose d'Or Award for International Format of the Year."

While this might seem innocuous, if Arthur would not have been able to make the show happen because of personnel, logistics and business operations issues, he would have not only damaged his reputation with the studio that financed the project but also had a major financial loss. However, he averted this because of his tenacity, constant search for solutions, and ability to manage what the crisis scientists call the 5 stages of a crisis, which producers experience on an almost daily basis given the overwhelmingly tendency for things to go wrong with a television show or movie with literally thousands of moving parts.[7] There is the need to accomplish the multi-tasking feat of the following: preventing multiple cameras and lights and hundreds if not thousands of pieces of necessary miscellaneous equipment (like sound stages, props, wardrobes, stunt gadgetry, etc.) from breaking at any moment; ensuring quality control over the proper amount of light; making sure all scenes get shot on time and on budget with hundreds of behind-the-scenes freelance workers trying to work in harmony together; trying to maximize the best performance from frequently uncooperative and antagonistic directors and actors; keeping the studios updated and at bay because of their micromanaging tendencies; and managing many other factors impacting whether an entertaining product will be the end result of all of this collective work.

In a nutshell, producers manage the **5 stages of a crisis: detection, preparation and prevention, containment, recovery, and learning from the crisis.**[8] Each stage of the crisis requires specific strategies and actions, and each stage can make or break a creative solution to an impending disaster.

For companies that have used divergent thinking and navigated their way through the 5 crisis steps like Harry and Arthur (and all of the other incredible producers we interviewed), the results have been phenomenal. Here are just a few examples to give you a better sense of how creative leaders in other industries have done it:

- In the late 1990s, Apple, Inc. was facing financial decline and struggling to compete against the likes of the Dells and Compaqs of the world.[9] So Apple embarked on their own divergent thinking and crisis prevention path: they brought Steve Jobs back from exile, launched a slew of new revolutionary products (including the iMac, iPod, and later iPhone, which reinvigorated their brand and sales), and transformed the company from irrelevant maker of computers to a must-have lifestyle brand that defines creativity.[10] All occurred because they turned around their crisis.

- Likewise, LEGO, Inc. was facing a similar crisis in the early 2000s due to a shift in children's play preferences and electronic toys.[11] But instead of continuing on their path into greater and greater decline, they introduced themed sets like LEGO Star Wars and LEGO Harry Potter— not an obvious idea that would inevitably work at the time. As a result, their entire business and fortunes were turned around for the better.[12]

- Lastly, in the late 2000s, Dominoes was facing a customer revolt due to dissatisfaction with the quality of their pizza.[13] Instead of pretending there wasn't a problem like many traditional leaders do (they often, in fact, gaslight customers and refuse to accept responsibility for crises of their own making)—they embarked on a "Pizza Turnaround" campaign. They acknowledged customer woes, introduced new recipes, and even improved their delivery service, saving and enhancing their sales and brand perception in the process. [14]

In other words, these companies used creative leadership and divergent thinking to stop their crises dead in their tracks. And not only did they successfully do this, but they managed to profit off of them too. What is the old saying by Winston Churchill? *Never let a good crisis go to waste.* Well, in this case it was true. Interestingly, research also shows that if a company manages their crises well like LEGO they can increase brand value by up to 22%. This can translate to millions or even billions of dollars in some cases[15]! Research also shows that if an organization handles its communication well like Dominoes did during a crisis it can increase consumer trust by up to 83%, translating to improved loyalties and sales as well.[16]

So the verdict is in: if you want to improve your own creative leadership skills, invest in your own divergent thinking, before, during, and after the inevitable crises of business. .

CASE STUDY: ANDREW CARLBERG'S CRISIS MANAGEMENT BLUEPRINT

In the film industry, crisis management often requires more than just quick thinking and resourcefulness; it necessitates a profound ability to navigate complex emotional and professional landscapes with prudent judgment and decision-making abilities. Andrew Carlberg, an Emmy® and Oscar® winning producer known for his prudent approach to crisis management, provides a compelling example of this during a pivotal moment in his career.

During the pre-production phase of one of Andrew's films, the project encountered severe complications. The film's development was faltering as key elements, such as securing financing and finalizing cast members, fell into disarray. At a critical juncture, a colleague whom he deeply respected pulled him aside and told him, "We need to know when not to make a movie. The universe is telling us we should not be making this movie right now." It wasn't what he wanted to hear, but he started to mull over the statement with deep seriousness.

Andrew knew he was facing a dilemma no successful producer like himself ever wants to be in: should he forge ahead despite the mounting issues or make the difficult decision to halt production? Not only would it be inconvenient to do this—getting a film greenlit in the first place has a less than 0.01% chance of happening—but it could cause reputation issues, problems with other financiers who previously committed funds to the project, complications with existing cast and crew members who had signed on, and beyond. But after thoughtfully considering how he made his decision, he told us, "Sometimes it is irresponsible to make a movie. Knowing when not to make a movie is just as important as knowing when to make a movie." Not only is this the very definition of ethical and practical leadership, but also of life wisdom: knowing not only *how* and *why* to do something, but *when* and *where* to do something—or not do something.

Faced with the potential collapse of the project, Andrew started to explore his options. Instead of adhering to the traditional approach of pushing through regardless of the circumstances—the hubristic approach many traditional leaders use to ignore reality and try to impose their will to try to "turn things around" like Lehman Brothers did in 2008 and Fyre Festival did in 2018—he examined the situation from multiple angles. He understood that the failure to secure necessary components was not merely a setback but a signal to reassess the project's viability.

So he started gathering input from his team one-by-one and critically evaluating all of his available options. As this was happening, he was influenced by a quote he came across from Ron Howard which said, "the best idea wins, but it's not a democracy." What he interpreted this to mean was that while it was essential to consider all perspectives, the final decision truly rested on his shoulders as the lead producer—the CEO of any Hollywood project.

The decision to therefore halt the project was not an easy one, especially given the emotional and financial investments already made—the equivalent of finishing all research and development, having a prototype designed, marketing the product to investors and future consumers, and then pulling the plug before it ever sees the light of day. However, Andrew's leadership and commitment to the project's integrity guided him through the process. He made the hard choice to cease production, understanding that proceeding under less-than-ideal conditions would compromise the final product and the well-being of everyone involved , not to mention compromise his credibility for potential future projects.

This decision was a testament to Andrew's capacity for leadership and his ability to prioritize the collective good over personal or financial interests. He reflected on the experience by emphasizing the importance of respecting every member of his team's interests and not just his own. "Anytime somebody disrespects any member of that community, they're disrespecting the whole process and the whole team," he notes. His decision to pause the project, though challenging, was driven by a respect for the team's contribution and a commitment to the project's long-term success , and the team's individual and personal long-term success.

Despite the challenges and difficult decisions made, he maintained an optimistic outlook. "There's so many movies that get made. And for that, there's literally 100,000 movies that don't get made," he reflects. His ability to accept and embrace these realities with grace and resilience demonstrates how he not only danced in the maze of crisis management, but how he has used wisdom and discretion to become one of the youngest winners of an Academy Award for other projects he's produced.

Key Takeaways

1. **Leadership Amidst Crisis**: Just as Harry Friedman, renowned producer of *Jeopardy!* and *Wheel of Fortune*, faced a pivotal moment during Hurricane Katrina, so too do creative leaders face multiple crises in their careers. Ultimately, quickly detecting and navigating each crisis can be critical. However, taking strategic advantage of each crisis is the hallmark of the most effective creative leaders.

2. **Divergent Thinking in Crisis Management**: Employing divergent thinking, typical in creative problem-solving, is essential in managing crises. With a mindset to swiftly

adapt, creative leaders can circumnavigate around operational and reputational disasters.

3. **Biological Impact of Crisis**: Crises can trigger significant stress (cortisol release), impacting decision-making, problem-solving, and interpersonal skills. Like Friedman, creative leaders can cultivate a familiarity with high-stakes decision-making to dampen these stressful impacts. Thus, clear-headed leadership can triumph during life-threatening situations or potential business disasters.

4. **Application Across Industries**: Similar crisis management skills are crucial across industries. Arthur Smith's experience producing "I Survived a Japanese Game Show" underscores the logistical challenges and critical decision-making necessary to avert financial and reputational crises.

5. **Strategic Crisis Management**: Successful crisis management involves stages like detection, preparation and prevention, containment, recovery, and learning. Examples from Apple, LEGO, and Domino's illustrate how companies turned crises into opportunities through innovative strategies and decisive actions.

CHAPTER 10

THE MENTOR MATRIX IS CALLING YOUR NAME

"He who can take advice is sometimes superior to him who can give it." [1]
— **Karl von Knebel**

Our Hollywood producers all agreed on one thing: their success in business, and in life, was dependent on the quality of advice they chose to listen to and follow—and the bad advice they chose to ignore.

They were on to something.

Producer Javier Chapa, whom we met briefly in the last chapter, believes this to his core. In fact, prior to becoming a producer, he was studying to become a lawyer and would have gone down that path (although that would not have made him happy) unless his mentor had not steered him away from it. He told us,

"I came from a family of lawyers and judges. And while I didn't go to law school for that reason, I thought it would be a good education for me to get...but I honestly spent more time studying film...I read books on editing, producing, you name it. I also clerked for one of the first Hispanic judges to be appointed to the bench, Bonito Garcia. And he said to me, 'listen, you're clearly not passionate about the practice of law. You should get out of here. He passed away a few months before I graduated and I took that as a sign and I took his words, got out of there, and came to Hollywood."

Had it not been for his late mentor's nudging, Javier doesn't believe he would have ever entered the entertainment industry—and gone on to build one of the largest Hispanic-focused media companies in Tinseltown.

Fanshen Cox also said if it wasn't for Matt Damon and Ben Afflek's advice to spread her wings, she wouldn't have stepped out on her own as a producer. The same is true for many of the others who point to a mentor who gave them the wisdom, perspective, encouragement, and psychological permission to become who they were destined to be.

But unfortunately, anywhere between 70% to 80% of people in surveys state they don't have mentors like the producers we interviewed who they can go to to get advice. [2] And for leaders, if they don't have multiple mentors—not just a single person—to whom they can go to get various perspectives (both inside and outside of their organizations), this can be dangerous. Not only does not getting feedback or advice lead to increased errors in decision making, but it diminishes the leaders' ability to accurately perceive reality, understand and motivate people, and lead from a place of optimism and curiosity.[3]

Producer Allison Grodner told us,

"You can't produce from a place of fear. The biggest successes and the biggest failures come from taking big creative swings and not being afraid to try new things or to keep the camera rolling even when it is uncomfortable. Unscripted production is such a rollercoaster ride because it is based on real people and real situations and is incredibly unpredictable. Early on, I think I was more fearless than I am now and I always have to remind myself of this."

Allison then mentioned one time she did remind herself to get feedback from mentors and to not be so cautious and take a chance,

"I did something most people thought was crazy and impossible: As part of a television documentary on teens and violence, I took a group of troubled and violent teens from Los Angeles to a wilderness experience in Colorado and then to Columbine High School only three months after the tragic school shooting. These kids sat face to face with the families and victims of unspeakable violence and were forever changed. It ended up being incredibly authentic and powerful anti-gun violence footage as these kids gained empathy and were forever changed. We took a chance and it could have been a disaster but it ended up being amazingly compelling television and, more importantly, a life changing and powerful message. Not producing from a place of fear is this same piece of advice that myself and the Big Brother team follow every day as we make a commitment to continue to try new creative twists and risks in order to keep our 23 year old series fresh and current. Not everything will succeed but we are committed to following through and not letting our personal doubts or the voices of the very opinionated fans stop us from trying new things."

Arthur Smith also learned from a mentor not to be so cautious by communicating like a traditional leader who often hoards information and seeks to control communication with their team.

"I believe in being honest and open as a boss. And I'm an over communicator. Whether I'm talking to a network partner or an employee at my own company, I always tell the truth. When I'm talking to a buyer, I believe that they're paying us to tell them the truth. To say what we're really thinking, and feeling, and to share our expertise. It's the way my company is set up. Everybody talks to everybody and no one's afraid to say anything to anyone, as long as they're sincere and respectful."

Yet how often have you heard this from a leader as successful as Arthur? Probably not frequently, which is why it's such important advice he learned and wanted to pass on to others who are building their creative leadership capacities. Being honest, communicating respectfully, and being genuinely sincere in the process of all business communication is what creates trust, increases loyalty, and improves performance in the long run.

- Harry Friedman agreed. He told us he learned from mentors that it's even okay to admit when you don't know something, one of the hardest but most fruitful things to do. Why? Because when you admit that you need help, both your team and mentors can chip in and offer their talent, experience, and perspective. In many cases, this is valuable. A hidden benefit is that you have created a de facto collaboration; now every contributor has a vested interest in helping to ensure that *their* idea or project succeeds. Interestingly, research shows that when leaders seek out advice about things they don't know—or even if they just want a second or third or fourth opinion—the following happens:

- Decisions improve in quality by 60%[4]

- Trust increases up to 460% by their colleagues[5]

- Their error rate is reduced by 30%[6]

In a study conducted by researcher Sousa Lobo and his team in 2005, when leaders have multiple opinions to help them navigate—a network of opinions, really—they are more successful.[7] But the key caveat the researchers mentioned is that this network of opinions does not have to be one of 'strong ties'; that is, a network of weak ties (of people you do not know very well and interact with only when you need to) help provide more novel perspectives, alternative solutions, and new opportunities than one's immediate circle. This network of opinions leads to stronger professional development, career advancement, and leadership success.[8] Of course, we frequently never hear this perspective because most of us have been told there is "one right" way for mentorship: having the "one right mentor" who is very close to us and who will singularly or exclusively help guide us, and give us good advice.

What About Bad Advice?

Of course, it's great when good advice is given from a single mentor, and especially better if it is given from a diverse group, but what about when bad advice is given? More specifically, what bad advice have these creative leaders heard that many traditional leaders take as gospel that they should avoid?

Harry Friedman shared 3 pieces of bad advice he thinks leaders should avoid like the plague: 1. "That it is better to be feared than to be liked"; 2. "That it's better to ask forgiveness than to ask for permission"; and 3. "Trust no one."

What's fascinating about what Harry is saying is just how much the scientific research aligns with what his personal experience—and over 60 Emmys® (between himself and his shows)—have taught him: that being feared leads to lower employee morale, lower productivity, lower creativity, lower problem solving, and higher turnover. The research also shows that asking for forgiveness and not permission leads to legal and ethical issues, strained trust and relationships, communication breakdowns, and strong risk of reputational damage. Finally, trusting no one leads to all of these aforementioned issues as well as a negative organizational culture and impaired decision making for others.

And even if the workplace you're in is toxic—and demonstrates all of these negative qualities—Laura Gutin says not to fall into the trap of letting this bad behavior get to you, coarsen you, diminish you, or cause you to be less than your best. Laura told us,

"Be nice. Not fake nice. But genuinely nice. It's so much better to be nice to people, and you get better results from them. For a long time in Hollywood, this wasn't the case. There was this belief that in order to get the best from people they have to be scared all of the time. And I think that's not true. Speaking as someone who came up being scared in a lot of Writers Rooms, it wastes a lot of your energy, just being scared, trying to triangulate, thinking what's going to happen, wondering if I'm going to get fired? But being nice doesn't mean you're not rigorous in your work, it does mean you're fostering a supportive environment."

Laura further went on to tell us when you're leaving an unsupportive environment, bad advice she's heard that she does not recommend: burning bridges.

"So even if you're leaving for whatever reason, your bosses or some people at your organization may still really like you. And that's a bridge you don't want to burn. I try to look at the place I'm leaving as just not the right fit, learn from my experiences there, and move on…if you decide the place was terrible and that you're going to burn it down, you put yourself in an unnecessarily vulnerable position. Now you're leaving with all of these people who could have recommended you but who instead say, na, they were really ugly, really nasty, they left a bad taste in our mouths. I know, I know it's a natural instinct to want to lash out at people, make the people who hurt you feel some hurt too. Do that with your friends over drinks. You have to remember that you meet the same people going up as you do coming down. Be nice. It will not hurt you. If you're not nice, it could definitely hurt you. And why would you want to make things harder for yourself in an already difficult industry?"

How to Ask For Advice

By now, you might be asking yourself, after all of this great advice given, what's the best way to ask for it in your own situation? You may not have access to mentors like some of our producers here—and you may not have a formal or effective workplace mentorship program like companies like Costco, Salesforce, Procter & Gamble, and Airbnb do—but you still have ways to get advice so you can see your problem, idea, strategy, or approach from multiple vantage points, the key to becoming a creative thinking leader.[9 - 12]

- But before recommending how you can do this, here are a few thoughts on how NOT TO DO THIS. So often, when people reach out they:

- Are overly vague or ambiguous in advice they're asking for, which doesn't allow for mentors to provide helpful responses that are specific and clear;

- Ignore or disregard past advice given, undermining motivation and appreciation that the mentor needs in order to continue providing access and advice;

- Ask in a confrontational or defensive manner, which hinders open and constructive feedback;

- Only seek advice to confirm pre-existing beliefs, limiting exposure to multiple options, creative thinking, and optimal outcomes; and

- Fail to follow up and provide appreciative feedback on how the advice was helpful, which will limit mentors' desire to provide it in the future.

That said, there are some great ways to go about regularly asking for advice and perspective to make yourself a more creative leader. These include the following:

- Showing vulnerability and humility, which makes mentors more likely to respond;

- Asking specific questions and making specific requests, helping to frame your request with clear details on the advice you're seeking;

- Asking for advice face-to-face rather than over email, Linkedin, or other avenues, which tends to lead to more thoughtful and comprehensive advice from mentors;

- Acknowledging mentors' expertise to increase their willingness to respond; and

- Following up by expressing gratitude and thanking them for their time.

By seeing advice in this way, you can build a network of mentors and advisers—both inside and outside of your organization, which can make all the difference between success and failure on your creative leadership journey.

Next, we turn to our final chapter on "Improvisational Intelligence," which we hope will help offer some valuable lessons in navigating an uncertain future.

CASE STUDY: JAVIER CHAPA'S INSIGHT: LEVERAGING WEAK MENTOR TIES FOR GROWTH

Javier Chapa's journey in the entertainment industry offers a compelling example of how effective mentorship can shape a successful career, especially for a member of the Hispanic community like himself which has been historically very underrepresented in Hollywood (by a factor of more than 10 to 1). As a prominent producer serving the LatinX market, Javier has navigated the changing complexities of the industry with a focus on surrounding himself with talented creatives, understanding the business of fundraising, and leading with empathy and respect.

One of Javier's core pieces of advice for both aspiring producers in entertainment and for (creative) leaders outside of Hollywood is to "surround yourself with really talented creatives who have skills you don't have. But don't try to boss them around or feel intimidated by them. Instead, play with each other's ideas and become a jazz ensemble by flowing with each other and making each other better. You can only succeed if you truly work together, not just have a bunch of creative people implement your ideas."

In addition to learning to trust others in collaborations—an insight he learned from his mentor, a federal judge—Javier also underscored the importance of mastering the art of raising money or securing financing if you want to be taken seriously as a creative leader and get things done. "I think you have to learn how to raise money," he advises, recognizing that financial independence is a significant factor in successful leadership of any type. In Bob and Rob's experience, they echo this sentiment—they have seen how it's often the people who are good with accessing capital who are the ones who get their projects made, not necessarily the people with the most creative ideas or most compelling cinematic ideas. Being able to secure funding for Javier allows him to have more control over his projects and avoid being "handcuffed or beholden to streamers or studios."

But even with this entrepreneurial mindset, Javier has found that navigating the challenges of raising capital—which is twice as hard for Latinx projects—can be a major challenge. So instead of going the traditional routes of many producers, he often finds innovative ways to secure resources for his projects outside of the Hollywood system by going to venture capital or private equity funds directly. This skill has not only provided him with the freedom to pursue his vision but also taught him the value of perseverance and creativity in overcoming financial hurdles—and helped him make the projects he wanted, many of which have become #1 hits on streamers across the globe.

More than anything else, though, Javier said the thing he learned the most from his mentors is about relationships. "You have to inspire people," he explains, noting that treating everyone on a set with respect—regardless of their position—is crucial. He acknowledges that while technical skills are important (and perhaps 20% of the job), the ability to connect with people and inspire them is what truly sets successful leaders apart (which is perhaps about 80% of the job). "You have to be really good with people and understand different people's needs."

Javier's ability to handle various personalities with tact and sensitivity reflects his broader philosophy of creative leadership. He acknowledges the challenges of managing egos and conflicts but views these as opportunities to protect the integrity of a project and foster a collaborative environment because he views the entertainment industry as a platform for the storytelling and creative expression that the world craves, and he wants to give it to them.

Key Takeaways

1. **The Power of Mentorship**: Successful Hollywood producers attribute much of their success to the quality of advice they received from mentors. Mentors provided wisdom, perspective, encouragement, and the psychological permission to pursue their true passions, steering them away from paths that would not have fulfilled them.

2. **Impact of Mentorship on Decision Making**: Having multiple mentors who provide diverse perspectives is crucial for leaders. It not only enhances decision-making quality by up to 60% but also increases trust from colleagues by 460%. Leaders who seek advice are better equipped to perceive reality accurately, understand and motivate people, and lead with optimism.

3. **Fearlessness in Leadership**: Effective producers emphasize the importance of fearlessness in leadership. Taking creative risks and maintaining openness to new ideas, even in unpredictable environments like unscripted television production, leads to both successes and failures. The willingness to innovate and push boundaries is crucial for staying relevant and impactful.

4. **Avoiding Bad Advice**: Producers warn against three common pieces of bad advice: a) It is better to be feared than liked; b) It's better to ask forgiveness than permission; c) Trust no one. These approaches can lead to lower morale, diminished trust, ethical dilemmas, and impaired decision-making abilities, ultimately undermining organizational effectiveness.

5. **Professional Conduct and Personal Integrity**: Maintaining honesty, openness, and sincerity in communication is essential for effective leadership. Leaders who communicate respectfully, give honest feedback, and admit when they don't know something foster trust, loyalty, and better performance within their teams and organizations.

CHAPTER 11

IMPROVISATIONAL INTELLIGENCE: REAL LEADERS BUILD THE PLANE AS THEY FLY IT

"The creative adult is the child who survived." [1]
— **Ursula K. Le Guin**

"The secret of change is to focus all of your energy not on fighting the old, but on building the new."
— **Socrates**

Producer Cybill Liu embodies what it means to bring all of the qualities of the creative leader together: curiosity, optimism, playfulness, leading through stories, building the right team, making difficult decisions, managing crises, and finally, intuitively imagining her way toward an improvised future. Not only did Cybill never plan—or hope—for a career in the entertainment business, for example, but her first career was just about as far from Hollywood (and creativity) as one could imagine: banking and finance.

But as Cybill was successfully working in finance (raising billions of dollars), she became increasingly more curious about entertainment. And as her curiosity grew, she started to learn more about it, optimistically concluding that she could succeed as a producer, and moved thousands of miles to Los Angeles to take her shot. She shut the door on her past, and looked forward to her new, less certain future.

What she found once she got there, however, was an unpredictable movie business, the instability of freelance work, and being exposed to individuals who didn't always have the purest of motives. She told us,

"You go into a movie with the best people you can find, with the best of intentions, but you'll find that people don't always represent themselves honestly, or can't do the work, but as a producer you have to see the project through."

In other words, what Cybill found was an industry laced with uncertainty that she had to frequently improvise her way through during unexpected down times if she wanted to be successful —something all creative leaders of any industry will have to do with the rapid acceleration of technological and workplace change.

Likewise, Lloyd J. Schwartz told us about a time he had to improve to save a shoot on the set of *The Brady Bunch*,

"There was an episode where Bob ("Mike Brady") was gonna teach the girls how to cook. And Florence ("Carol Brady") was going to play baseball with the boys. So it was a switch of traditional parenting roles type of story. And I'm standing there on the set and I watch the wardrobe people come to Florence and give her a completely uppity and inappropriate outfit.

"She looked over at the director and said to him, 'I can't play in these clothes.' She was in pants and needed a shirt to play the scene. And she then looked around, spotted me, and said,

Lloyd, give me your shirt. So I gave my shirt to Florence and then we did the scene. And I'm bare chested without a shirt and I feel kind of awkward standing on the set that way. Once they finished filming, I asked, can I have my shirt back? They said no, in case they have to do a re-shoot or something. I never saw my shirt again but we did get the shot that we needed."

Interestingly, surveys of workplace adults across fields indicate that over 84% of employees have been recently asked to improvise just like Lloyd in their current job—and, at least to us and most observers, this improvisation will only increase in its frequency.[3]

Stephanie Drachkovitch, who has had more than 20 different television shows aired in 120+ countries, underscores this point and humbly credits intuition and improvisation for her massive success. She said,

"What most people think is true about being in Hollywood and being a leader here is that we must know more than other people, but really we don't know anything! Sometimes we forget that our whole business is just a best-guess business. We do have the introduction of data and analytics that we didn't have when I first started, so yes, we can look at trends, an algorithm and look at hard data, but I think sometimes there's this assumption that because we have the big job, we must really know more than everybody else. But we don't know that much more. It's our observations, our opinions, it's our instincts, it's our taste, and it's our curiosity, not our superiority to others."

What Stephanie is highlighting not only for creative leaders in Hollywood, but for leaders everywhere is the notion that just because you're in charge doesn't mean you know everything—or even know that much or the best path forward. There are definitely traces of Aristotle in her spot on thinking, as the philosopher said thousands of years ago, "The more you know, the more you realize you don't know."

What's even more telling about Stephanie's insights—which our other producers acknowledged as well—is how much this perspective is not only philosophical in nature, but backed by hard data. People who think they're experts, according to researchers, usually almost always make wrong predictions![4] It turns out that experience not only frequently leads to overconfidence bias, rigidity in thinking, and various cognitive biases, but also counterintuitively creates an unwillingness to learn from mistakes and diminished ability to incorporate diverse perspectives other than one's own. But many experienced traditional leaders deny this—even though the science is compelling and overwhelming. Put differently, many experienced leaders deny the idea that what they know might not be serving them or their teams, or might not be as much as they think they know.

Regardless, this may soon be a moot point for many industries as artificial intelligence (AI) is increasingly able to predict numerous outcomes with accuracy, rendering experience less and less important anyway. For example, in everything from the prediction of stock prices, healthcare diagnostics on a range of medical conditions, legal outcomes in litigation, human resources for identifying high potential employees, and cybersecurity, among other areas, AI will make it that much more crucial for a leader to be improvisational, intuitive, and even imaginative, not just experienced and credentialed. In many industries of business, trying to predict and manage the future will count for less and less.[5 6 7 8 9]

In Richard and Daniel Susskind's seminal book, *The Future of the Professions: How Technology Will Transform The Work of Human Experts*, they take this idea a step further by arguing that AI will also radically disrupt not just outcomes but also the workflow in domains that were once assumed untouchable.[10] Technology be able to do much of the substantive work lawyers, doctors, and accountants used to do. With changing customer demands and new online services, the democratic spread of once highly-guarded knowledge will be inevitable. The erosion of credentials (and credential-granting bodies like universities and professional associations) may be inescapable. And the seasoned traditional leader may face certain extinction.[11]

This is why, again, it is so paramount to learn and practice the mindsets and skillsets of creative leadership, particularly learning to, and being comfortable with, improvising.

But it's not just survival on the line. Part of improvising can be having to do—or be—something in the moment that might seem trivial relative to existential concerns but can still be terrifying nonetheless. This improvising will spell the difference between success or failure, or even you or your project's reputation. Arthur Smith told us,

"We were filming *Hell's Kitchen* in Vegas and we had this 2,000 seat theater. We're all in the control room and we're about to unveil our show and I go, 'When is the warm up guy going out there?' 'Well,' somebody said, 'there is no warm up guy. We don't have a warm up.' And I said, 'What do you mean we don't have a warm up, we need a warmup to get the audience engaged because every live show needs one'. So I decided on the spot, OK, give me the mic." I would have been kind of nervous, but I have a background in performing; however, I'm not a stand up comedian; I'm not a warm up guy. If I would have thought about the fact that I have to perform in front of 2,000 people in Vegas, I probably would have been a lot more nervous and crazy instead of just doing it, so I went out and I played Vegas on the spot. I told jokes about Gordon [Ramsay], *Hell's Kitchen* and I brought people up from the audience. I completely winged it. And Gordon, the crew, and thankfully the audience were laughing."

While this is a fun, once-in-a-lifetime and dramatic story Arthur shared, the point is still well taken: when it comes to many things as a leader, especially when something falls through or is not going according to plan, you don't have time to overthink, overanalyze, or wait for the best (or worst) to happen—you have to do something now, letting your intuition and imagination guide you. What's stunning is that when a leader personally models this behavior like Arthur did by letting intuition and imagination take a front seat, it sends a powerful message to their team that 1) spontaneity and creativity are valued; 2) non-linear thinking can be a solution; and 3) adaptation can lead to success. This message is often even returned in-kind by team members. According to a study by Deloitte, organizations with strong intuition and imagination are 500% more likely to have higher productivity and financial growth. Arthur's show is evidence of this—as it is one of the highest grossing shows of all time.

But it's not just in the realm of a fast moving decision that improvisation can be beneficial; it can be helpful in other ways too.

For example, Hollywood itself was faced with the choice of improvising (and changing) how it hires its workforce and getting higher return on investment as a result—or sticking with its current operating structure when Producer Fanshen Cox imagined a new future for it. As Fanshen, who is part Jamaican and part white, told us, one of the things she noticed working in Hollywood was that there were not very many women directors (less than 10% of total directors at the time) and people of color writers or producers (also less than 10% at the time), which she thought was very unfair.[12-14] So she decided she wanted to even the playing field and create a new, better Hollywood. She said,

"You know, growing up with Ben [Affleck] and Matt [Damon] as friends was such a blessing. We started to have this conversation around how we make sure that Hollywood has true equality of opportunity when it comes to who gets to tell stories. It was based on this idea that talent is evenly distributed, but opportunity is not, especially in an industry that relies on who you know. And they were very, very supportive and said we should figure this out. So one day I reached out to Dr. Stacy Smith at USC, who was doing a lot of work around representation, and Kalpana Kotagal (a renowned labor attorney), and we created this thing called the 'Inclusion Rider,' to make sure Hollywood sets would hire people from all walks of life— so we could increase the number of female directors, people of color, among other things. And Ben and Matt decided to put the Inclusion Rider in their movies to set a positive example. For instance, they used it in making the movie *Air* they made about Michael Jordan. And now many other production companies have done it too and we're starting to see gradual change."

What's clear from Fanshen's experience, as well as Arthur and Cybill's, is that their ability to improvise has been one of the primary tools they've used to survive, thrive, and re-shape reality. Whether it be to save a project, keep a show moving, or advocate for change, using their intuition and imagination has been very useful.

Increasing Intuition, Improvisation, and Imagination In Your Leadership

But the question that you might have is, how can you do this in your own creative leadership? How can you use intuition, imagination, and improvisation?

Before we lay out a few ways for you to practice this, Cybill wanted to share an important principle to keep in mind. Even though she has had top box office hits on Netflix and other streaming platforms that have been # 1 in dozens of countries, she told us,

"It is not necessary for you to have one huge accomplishment, but instead a series of smaller accomplishments. When you become more intrinsically motivated as a leader about enjoying the journey, seeing where it takes you and what not, the easier it will be for you to overcome constant obstacles with fresh thinking and more joy."

We agree. You will not only put less pressure on yourself of having to do one big thing—or the next big thing—but you will free yourself to be more creative because you're not so focused on the result but rather savoring experimenting with the long journey. Here are just a few ways:

1. **Like with curiosity, exposing yourself to different ideas, unique ways of thinking, different cultural experiences, different industries, and people from various socioeconomic backgrounds (with different education, income, geographic perspectives than you) will help your intuition.**[15] Even better, by reflecting on your exposure to these, your gut instincts and hunches will sharpen because your interpretative lenses of the world will be wider and more accurate. You will not just be relying on your own narrow lived experience to lead; instead, you will be incorporating a more holistic human experience by utilizing the best of others' learnings and successes.

2. **Role play from various perspectives during brainstorming, mindmapping, and free writing exercises.**[16] For example, if you brainstorm about solutions from the perspective of other personality types, professionals in different industries, or even different roles in your own organization, you'd be surprised at how divergent—and imaginative—your thinking can become. You will also be surprised at how much your empathy and emotional intelligence increases too. So don't just brainstorm, role play while doing it.

3. **Engage in actual improv classes and team improv exercises.**[17] Through training your brain to think—and more

importantly, act—on the spot, you can become more comfortable in doing these things as a creative leader. But the trick is to not do it just as a one-off, unique experience; continually invest in this skill throughout your career as a way to make yourself much quicker on your feet –in terms of how you think, speak, act, and react.

CASE STUDY: CYBILL LIU'S MASTERY OF IMPROVISATIONAL INTELLIGENCE IN LEADERSHIP

In the ever-shifting landscape of Hollywood, where uncertainty is a constant and the only guarantee is change, Cybill Liu shines as a beacon of improvisational intelligence. Her journey from the structured world of billion dollar financial deals on Wall Street to the unpredictable realm of film production is a testament to her adaptability and creative acumen as a leader. After all, it's not common for somebody to know how to transition from successfully managing equity, debt, and private placements to managing fragile artistic types—and even more fragile artistic endeavors—that have landed in the Top Ten most viewed Netflix projects in over 50 countries.

Cybill's story begins far from the glittering lights of Los Angeles, in the rigorous and disciplined world of finance. Raised amidst spreadsheets and balance sheets, she was a master at raising cash and managing financial portfolios for telecom groups and even radiotherapy cancer treatment facilities. Yet, as successful as she was, her curiosity for entertainment grew, an ember glowing in the background of her high-stakes career. Her decision to transition into the entertainment industry was driven by a blend of optimism and curiosity about how she could integrate the rational side of her brain (that managed numbers and budgets and logistics) with her equally powerful but underutilized creative side (that understands story and human emotion). She concluded that if you want to become all that you're destined to be—and not live with "golden handcuffs" the rest of your life—"You have to shut the door on your past to open the door to a new future even if you don't know what that future will look like."

But the world of Hollywood was nothing like the predictable realm of finance. It was a landscape fraught with uncertainty, filled with freelance instability and individuals whose true motives were not always transparent. Cybill found herself in a world where even the most meticulously planned projects could unravel unexpectedly. She told us, "There are many people who claim to have a perfect resume but when you get on set, they don't know how to use it if the conditions and circumstances are different from what they've previously been in. Or there are people who just make stuff up, don't have the skills and experiences they say they have, don't follow through when they've committed money to your project, or even forge your signature to get money for themselves." Put differently, there are many people looking to take advantage of people to help themselves, which underscores why improvisational intelligence is even more important to keep yourself—and your team—safe.

Despite facing charlatans—endemic to every industry, as fraud is a $1 trillion dollar a year business in the United States according to the Association of Certified Fraud Examiners—Cybill has been able to shepherd projects ranging from *Casino Jack* to *The Girl Who Invented Kissing* and beyond to top film festivals, top streaming sites, and beyond. Projects that have not only been nominated for Best Picture but also have been commercially at the top of the charts around the world.

But Cybill cautions all leaders with this sage advice: "It is not necessary for you to have one huge accomplishment, but instead a series of smaller accomplishments." In other words, you don't have to have one big win, one big thing you're known for, one big goal that you feel if you reach your life is complete. Instead, you can live life, rack up many doubles and triples with a few singles and occasional home runs thrown in there. Being able to work on many projects with varying degrees of market popularity frees leaders from obsessing over always being number 1 or the idea that being number 1 is synonymous with the only true way to be successful (the one right way model that traps traditional leaders in their tracks).

In a world increasingly shaped by artificial intelligence and technological advancements, the ability to improvise will only become more crucial. The rise of AI means that traditional expertise and experience may no longer be as valuable as they once were. For leaders like Cybill, this means that improvisational intelligence—combining intuition, creativity, and adaptability—will be essential for thriving in an ever-changing environment.

Cybill's journey, along with the insights shared by other industry leaders, underscores a vital lesson for all creative leaders: embrace uncertainty, trust your instincts, and remain adaptable. The path to success is often paved with unforeseen challenges and opportunities that require quick thinking and a willingness to improvise. This perspective not only enriches the creative process but also fosters resilience and adaptability, key traits for navigating the unpredictable world of leadership.

Key Takeaways

1. **Embracing Uncertainty and Change**: Creative leaders like Cybill Liu and Stephanie Drachkovitch highlight the necessity of navigating uncertainty in their careers. Cybill, originally from finance, transitioned to entertainment driven by her curiosity and optimism, despite the unpredictable nature of the industry. Her adaptation to change and improvisation underscores the importance of flexibility and resilience in leadership.

2. **Intuition Over Experience**: Stephanie Drachkovitch challenges the notion that leadership is about having all the answers. She emphasizes that effective leadership often

relies more on intuition, curiosity, and adaptability rather than traditional expertise or experience. This perspective encourages leaders to trust their instincts and embrace a more fluid approach to problem-solving and decision-making.

3. **Importance of Improvisation**: Arthur Smith's experience during the filming of *"Hell's Kitchen"* exemplifies the critical role of improvisation in leadership. When faced with unexpected challenges like the absence of a warm-up act before a live show, Smith relied on spontaneity and creativity to engage the audience successfully. This demonstrates that effective leadership requires the ability to think on one's feet and make quick, informed decisions under pressure.

4. **Promoting Diversity and Inclusion**: Fanshen Cox's advocacy for the Inclusion Rider in Hollywood illustrates how leaders can use improvisational thinking to drive positive change. By challenging the status quo and advocating for diversity in film production, Cox showcases how leaders can leverage their influence to shape industry standards and foster inclusivity.

5. **Continuous Learning and Adaptation**: The discussion on the impact of artificial intelligence (AI) underscores the need for leaders to continuously learn and adapt. As AI disrupts traditional roles and practices across various industries, leaders who cultivate improvisational intelligence—combining intuition, imagination, and adaptability—will be better equipped to navigate and capitalize on these changes.

CONCLUSION

"Life is a series of conclusions, each one leading to another beginning."
—Bob Boden & Dr. Rob Carpenter

As many creative leaders say when they reach the end of their project: "this is our curtain call," or the time to wrap things up. But we certainly hope you have enjoyed this book, learned from it, and are able to apply its insights and lessons practically in your own leadership journey. Below please find a brief summary of its key concepts to help refresh your memory and to use as you discuss creative leadership with those around you—and utilize in hands-on ways.

There is No One Right Way To Lead, Solve Problems, Or Accomplish Things

Despite education systems and traditional leaders insisting that there is "only one right answer"—similar to the "one right answer" for math equations or science formulas or standardized tests like the SAT—in creative leadership there is no such thing. The black-and- white thinking of the past, the right or wrong categorical approaches, the idea that you're not allowed to see the world in multiple colors—are outdated and destructive. Creative leaders understand that there are many different ways to skin a cat, and do not believe or demand that their way is always synonymous with "the way." This is creative intelligence at its finest, and recognizes that it is okay to blend multiple intelligences (thinking and feeling, among several others) together to create new things.

Curiosity Allows You To Transcend The Limits People, Workplaces, Or Society Tries To Put On You—And Come Up With Original Ideas And Solutions

Simply put, being curious, asking "what if," and genuinely seeking out new information and connections between seemingly different things is what creative leadership is about. Because society focuses so much on specialization, however, curiosity often declines as expertise increases, causing blind spots and the inability to break beyond myopic thinking. But even if you're an expert, or have ample experience, curiosity can be exercised through constant exposure to ideas, people, and experiences outside of your comfort zone, which will help you take ideas from one industry and apply them to another—the exact definition of creative innovation and what made Steve Jobs so effective.

OPTIMISM IS THE SINGLE MOST EFFECTIVE Leadership Style On The Planet

Machiavelli was wrong: it is not better to be feared, which many pessimistic and some realistic leaders believe. In reality, the best leaders are optimistic—about their plans, the capabilities of their people, and in how they communicate and solve problems—and always put plans in place in case the worst happens. Their most important contribution to their workplace is that they create positive environments, understand how to inspire and motivate people, and how to quickly recover from setbacks, something neither pessimistic or realistic leaders know how to do well according to mountains of scientific literature.

Playfulness Is A Significantly Missing Ingredient In Most Workplaces Today

Because there are so many challenges in the workplace (and wider world), many traditional leaders dismiss the idea that being playful could yield positive benefits for their teams, performance, or return on investment. As a consequence, they think that being fun or playful is naive and frivolous, to their unfortunate detriment. Research shows that leaders who are light-hearted, who don't take themselves too seriously, and who like to have a little bit of fun get better performance, better results from their team, and better bottom lines than those who don't.

Storytelling Is A Creative Leader's Superpower Because It Literally Changes Their Audience's Brain

The most important communication skill for any creative leader is their ability to tell compelling stories to motivate their team, their customers, and the wider world. They do this because they understand that when people hear a story, they can transmit the emotion they are personally feeling directly to their audiences' brains—and alter them to respond positively in kind. In other words, creative leaders understand the neuroscientific underpinnings of stories and how this ancient practice is quintessentially the most effective tool to build buy-in for nearly anything they're doing, provided that they have their facts and other ducks in a row.

It's The People Who Are Different From You Who Will Make Or Break Your Success

Workplace statistics throughout society demonstrate that most traditional leaders hire those that are just like them—similar educational backgrounds, similar personalities, similar looks, and the like. These statistics also show that this approach holds most organizations back because there is far too much similarity in their workplace DNA and not enough difference, resulting in creative and financial underperformance for organizations that are homogeneous in nature. On the other hand, the most creative leaders in the world recognize that diverse teams outperform homogeneous teams on every possible workplace metric and so therefore carefully recruit, hire, protect, and cultivate differences in their workplaces.

Healthy Competition With Yourself And Your Team Will Make You Better; Unhealthy Competition Will Leave You Bitter And Broken

The purpose of competition is not to win; the purpose is to become better and, ultimately, the best you can be. At times, this will be enough to allow you to win but at other times it won't. That's life and how the world works. That is why creative leaders embrace the idea that competition is all about improvement, not just about end results. For when they make competition about improvement and not just beating others, they protect themselves from the often bitter aftereffects of unhealthy competition, which includes: mental and emotional anguish, damaged relationships, physical health deterioration, and a destroyed reputation in the long-run for trying to win at all costs.

Without A Decision-Making Framework, Your Decisions Will Often Result In Failure

One of the largest blind spots for traditional leaders is their overconfidence about believing they almost always make the right decisions. Part of the reason for this is because of their various cognitive biases they're unaware of, which negatively impact 8 out of every 10 decisions and often result in costly misfires. This is why it is crucial for leaders, especially creative ones who are dealing with more and more uncertainty, to have science-based decision frameworks in place they can use to mitigate the errors in the judgments they will inevitably make regardless of their experience or educational backgrounds.

Your Organization Will Experience A Crisis Every Few Years And You Can't Panic When It Happens

Given the rate of accelerated change and upheaval in society today, every workplace will experience an organizational or industry-wide crisis that could bring it existentially to its knees from time to time. This means that just because there was a crisis 3 years ago and it was weathered does not mean there will not be another one tomorrow that is vastly different. Crises can often be diverted but they are impossible to plan for, given how many variables are out of an organization's control. For each crisis, the most creative leaders understand how to creatively solve them before it's too late as every crisis requires new ideas and solutions, not just dusting off the old playbook of the past.

It's Mentors You Don't Know Well Who Will Open More Doors For You Than The Ones You Do

The prototypical image of a mentor is somebody who is more advanced and successful and who will, through an email, phone call, or lunch or dinner, change your life in an instant. And while this does happen for creative leaders at times, the reality is less cinematic: most of the most successful people in society neither have a single mentor, or mentors who they know deeply, who help navigate them through the vicissitudes of their careers. Instead, they build a network of "weak-tie" mentors that they don't know well but who they occasionally engage to help them propel forward. For creative leaders, the ones with the biggest network of weak-tie mentors win in the long-run, not just the one with a single great mentor.

Nothing Is Guaranteed; You Have To Improvise Your Way Through Life And Leadership

As many of our Hollywood producers have shown us, the only thing guaranteed in creative leadership is that you will have to improvise. That is, you will have to create, re-direct, plan again, change what you are doing, and generally always be ready to ad-lib your way through the various precarious acts of leadership. Because the world is getting less certain and less predictable, the thing that you must get very good at is not only going with the flow but figuring out multiple ways to successfully direct the flow depending on which way it's running.

LAST WORDS

Throughout this book, you have heard from multiple Hollywood producers who have let you into the secrets of their success—and the secrets of creative leadership. These producers have numerous Oscars®, Emmys®, Grammys®, and beyond, have collectively produced tens of thousands of episodes of television and movies, and navigated the most statistically competitive industry in the world. Their insights about creative intelligence, curiosity, optimism, playfulness, storytelling, competition, decision making, crisis management, the role of mentors, and improvising in high stakes scenarios are not only invaluable, they are essential. Because Hollywood producers strategically manage uncertainty using both logic and intuition, their skillset will be more needed in every industry in America (and the world) as we enter an age where it is no longer possible to be successful by employing the traditional rules of the game. Instead, we are entering a world where you have to be as creative, innovative, and original as possible if you want to thrive much less survive. We hope you embrace this message and, even as you chew on it, that you recognize that what we've said throughout these pages is just one way to think about and approach creative leadership—but not the only way. As you continue to build your own creative intelligence, you will discover that there are multiple right paths and approaches to lead you forward. And there are more right paths and approaches after that, with a never-ending process of discovery and rediscovery, and a never-ending process of beginning again.

NOTES

Introduction

1. *Einstein, A. Creativity is intelligence having fun. Goodreads. Retrieved August 22, 2024, from* https://www.goodreads.com/quotes/37706-creativity-is-intelligence-having-fun

2. *The Creative Dividend: How Creativity Impacts Business Results.* Accessed from: https://www.americansforthearts.org/by-program/reports-and-data/legislation-policy/naappd/the-creative-dividend-how-creativity-impacts-business-results#:~:text=Our%20survey%20showed%20that%20creative,by%20a%20factor%20of%201.5.

3. Solomons, M. (2023, November 24). *Linearity Publication 70 Creativity Statistics: Work, School, and More.* Retrieved from: https://www.linearity.io/blog/creativity-statistics/

Chapter One

1. Angelou, M. (n.d.). *You can't use up creativity. The more you use, the more you have.* Goodreads. Retrieved August 22, 2024, from https://www.goodreads.com/quotes/153929-you-can-t-use-up-creativity-the-more-you-use-the

2. Andersen, E. (2022, April 7). *Change is hard. Here's how to make it less painful.* Harvard Business Review. https://hbr.org/2022/04/change-is-hard-heres-how-to-make-it-less-painful

3. Nussbaum, E. (2024, June 15). *How the real world created modern reality TV*. The New Yorker. https://www.newyorker. com/culture/the-weekend-essay/how-the-real-world-created-modern-reality-tv

4. Gardner, H. (1983). *Frames of Mind: The Theory of Multiple Intelligences*. Basic Books.

5. Borghans, L., Golsteyn, B. H. H., Heckman, J. J., & H., J. E. (2016, November). *What grades and achievement tests measure* (IZA Discussion Paper No. 10356). Institute of Labor Economics (IZA). https://docs.iza.org/dp10356.pdf

6. American Psychological Association. (2010). *Research in brain function and learning: Applications of psychological science to teaching and learning modules*. https://www.apa.org/ education-career/k12/brain-function#:~:text=In%20 fact%2C%20we%20now%20know,ready%20at%20 an%20earlier%20age

7. Ashby, F. G., Turner, B. O., & Horvitz, J. C. (2010). *Cortical and basal ganglia contributions to habit learning and automaticity*. Frontiers in Psychology, *1*, Article 27. https://www.ncbi.nlm. nih.gov/pmc/articles/PMC2862890/

8. Anthony, S. D., & Schwartz, E. I. (2017, May 8). *What the best transformational leaders do*. Harvard Business Review. https://hbr.org/2017/05/what-the-best-transformational-leaders-do

Chapter Two

1. Hobbes, T. (n.d.). *Curiosity is the lust of the mind*. Goodreads. Retrieved August 22, 2024, from https://www.goodreads. com/quotes/266024-curiosity-is-the-lust-of-the-mind

2. Waldrop, M. (2017, February 3). *Inside Einstein's love affair with 'Lina'—his cherished violin*. National Geographic. https://www.nationalgeographic.com/adventure/article/ einstein-genius-violin-music-physics-science

3. British Red Cross. (n.d.). *Marie Curie, the Red Cross, invisible light, and WWI*. Retrieved August 22, 2024, from https://www.redcross.org.uk/stories/our-movement/our-history/marie-curie-invisible-light-the-red-cross-and-wwi#:~:text=She%20was%20soon%20named%20director,is%20Marie%20Curie%20so%20famous%3F

4. Davis, L. (2013, May 19). *The unexpected artwork of physicist Richard Feynman*. Gizmodo. https://gizmodo.com/the-unexpected-artwork-of-physicist-richard-feynman-508717317

5. Time. (1964, January 3). *America's Gandhi: Rev. Martin Luther King Jr*. Time. https://content.time.com/time/subscriber/article/0,33009,940759-11,00.html#:~:text=King%20likes%20to%20play%20the,for%2045%20minutes%20of%20reading

6. Roberts, M. (2021, February 16). *Meet Coretta Scott King, a soprano and violinist who used music in her civil rights campaigning*. Classic FM. https://www.classicfm.com/discover-music/martin-luther-king-wife-coretta-scott-was-soprano-violinist/

7. Ahmed, W. (2019). *The Polymath: Unlocking the Power of Human Versatility*. Bloomsbury Publishing.

8. Ibid.

9. Pashler, H., & Wagenmakers, E.-J. (2012). Editors' introduction to the special section on replicability in psychological science: A crisis of confidence? *Perspectives on Psychological Science, 7*(6), 528-530. https://www.jstor.org/stable/44282601

10. Harvey, S. B., Epstein, R. M., Glozier, N., Petrie, K., Strudwick, J., Gayed, A., Dean, K., & Henderson, M. (2021, September 10). *Mental illness and suicide among physicians. BMJ, 374*, n. pag. https://www.ncbi.nlm.nih.gov/pmc/arti-

cles/PMC9618683/#:~:text=Notably%2C%20there%20
is%20emerging%20evidence,of%20suicide%20than%20
other%20specialists.

11. Bullock, O. M., Colón Amill, D., Shulman, H. C., & Dixon, G. N. (2019). Jargon as a barrier to effective science communication: Evidence from metacognition. *Public Understanding of Science, 28*(7), 845-853. https://pubmed.ncbi.nlm.nih.gov/31354058/#:~:text=We%20find%20that%20the%20presence,;%20processing%20fluency;%20science%20communication

12. Muro, M., Whiton, J., & Maxim, R. (2019, November 20). What jobs are affected by AI? Better-paid, better-educated workers face the most exposure. Brookings. https://www.brookings.edu/articles/what-jobs-are-affected-by-ai-better-paid-better-educated-workers-face-the-most-exposure/

13. Epstein, D. (2019). *Range: Why Generalists Triumph in a Specialized World.* Riverhead Books.

14. Catmull, E. (2014). *Creativity, Inc.: Overcoming the unseen forces that stand in the way of true inspiration.* Random House.

15. Grazer, B., & Fishman, C. (2015). *A Curious Mind: The Secret to a Bigger Life.* Simon & Schuster.

16. Baer, J. (2012). *The Curious Mind: The Secret to a Bigger Life.* Penguin Books.

17. Chevallier, A., Dalsace, F., & Barsoux, J.-L. (2024, May–June). *The art of asking smarter questions: These five techniques can drive great strategic decision-making.* Harvard Business Review. https://hbr.org/2024/05/the-art-of-asking-smarter-questions

18. Seel, N. M., & Massaro, D. W. (2012). *Multimodal learning.* In *Encyclopedia of the sciences of learning* (pp. 2203-2205). Spring-

er Science+Business Media. https://doi.org/10.1007/978-1-4419-1428-6_273

19. Poulopoulos, D. (2020, October 4). *Use the brute-force learning technique to gain new skills: Study new developments, stay up to date and conquer new knowledge with one simple trick.* Towards Data Science. https://towardsdatascience.com/use-the-brute-force-learning-technique-to-gain-new-skills-3f2fda6f0e7d

20. Kelly, J. (2012, September). *Learning pyramid.* Peak Performance Center. https://thepeakperformancecenter.com/educational-learning/learning/principles-of-learning/learning-pyramid/

21. Eurich, T. (2017). *Insight: The Surprising Truth About How Others See Us, How We See Ourselves, and Why the Answers Matter More Than We Think.* Currency.

22. Hamel, G. (2011, December). *First, let's fire all the managers.* Harvard Business Review. https://hbr.org/2011/12/first-lets-fire-all-the-managers

23. DiGangi, J. (2023, September–October). *The anxious micromanager: Why some leaders become too controlling and how they find the right balance.* Harvard Business Review. https://hbr.org/2023/09/the-anxious-micromanager

Chapter Three

1. Chomsky, N. *Optimism is a strategy for making a better future. Because unless you believe that the future can be better, you are unlikely to step up and take responsibility for making it so.* Goodreads. Retrieved August 22, 2024, from https://www.goodreads.com/quotes/158840-optimism-is-a-strategy-for-making-a-better-future-because

2. Humphrey, R. H. (2002). "The impact of emotional contagion on leadership effectiveness." *Journal of Organizational Behavior, 23*(7), 703-721. DOI: 10.1002/job.157

3. Judge, T. A., & Bono, J. E. (2001). *Relationship of core self-eval-uations traits—self-esteem, generalised self-efficacy, locus of control, and emotional stability—with job satisfaction and job performance: A meta-analysis. Journal of Applied Psychology, 86*(1), 80-92. DOI: 10.1037/0021-9010.86.1.80

4. Totterdell, P., & Holman, D. (2003). *Emotion regulation in the workplace: Test of a model of emotional labor. Journal of Applied Psychology, 88*(3), 493-507. DOI: 10.1037/0021-9010.88.3.493

5. Spector, P. E., & Fox, S. (2005). *The stressor-emotion model of counterproductive work behavior. In C. L. Cooper & E. A. Locke (Eds.), Industrial and organizational psychology: Linking theory with practice (pp. 129-154). Wiley*

6. *Lencioni, P. (2002). The five dysfunctions of a team: A leadership fable. Jossey-Bass*

7. *Kirkpatrick, S. A., & Locke, E. A. (1996). Direct and indi-rect effects of three core charismatic leadership components on perfor-mance and attitudes. Journal of Applied Psychology, 81(1), 36-51. https://doi.org/10.1037/0021-9010.81.1.36*

8. Locke, E. A., & Latham, G. P. (2002). *Building a practically useful theory of goal setting and task motivation: A 35-year od-yssey. American Psychologist, 57*(9), 705-717. https://doi.org/10.1037/0003-066X.57.9.705

9. Locke, E. A., & Latham, G. P. (2002). *Building a practically useful theory of goal setting and task motivation: A 35-year od-yssey. American Psychologist, 57*(9), 705-717. https://doi.org/10.1037/0003-066X.57.9.705

10. Conversano, C., Rotondo, A., Lensi, E., Della Vista, O., Arpone, F., & Reda, M. A. (2010). Optimism and its impact on mental and physical well-being. *National Library of Med-icine.* Retrieved from https://www.ncbi.nlm.nih.gov/pmc/articles/PMC2894461/

11. Ibid.

12. Ibid.

13. Fredrickson, B. L., & Losada, M. F. (2005). Positive affect and the complex dynamics of human flourishing. *American Psychologist, 60*(7), 678-686. https://doi.org/10.1037/0003-066X.60.7.678

14. Zhao, H., & Seibert, S. E. (2006). *The Big Five personality dimensions and entrepreneurial status: A meta-analytic review. Journal of Applied Psychology, 91*(2), 259-271. https://doi.org/10.1037/0021-9010.91.2.259

15. Conversano, C., Rotondo, A., Lensi, E., Della Vista, O., Arpone, F., & Reda, M. A. (2010). Optimism and its impact on mental and physical well-being. *National Library of Medicine.* Retrieved from https://www.ncbi.nlm.nih.gov/pmc/articles/PMC2894461/

16. Arbinger Institute. (2010). *Leadership and self-deception: Getting out of the box.* Berrett-Koehler Publishers.

17. McCrae, R. R., & Costa, P. T. (1997). *Personality trait structure as a human universal. American Psychologist, 52*(5), 509-516. https://doi.org/10.1037/0003-066X.52.5.509

18. Emmons, R. A., & McCullough, M. E. (2003). *Counting blessings versus burdens: An experimental investigation of gratitude and subjective well-being in daily life. Journal of Personality and Social Psychology, 84*(2), 377-389. https://doi.org/10.1037/0022-3514.84.2.377

19. Losada, M., & Heaphy, E. D. (2004). *The role of positivity and connectivity in the performance of business teams: A nonlinear dynamics model. American Behavioral Scientist, 47*(6), 740-765. https://doi.org/10.1177/0002764203260208

20. Grant, A. M., & Parker, S. K. (2009). *Redesigning work design theories: The rise of relational and proactive perspectives.*

Academy of Management Annals, 3(1), 317-375. https://doi. org/10.5465/19416520903047327

21. McDonald, T., & Gergen, K. J. (2010). *Comparing solution-focused brief therapy and cognitive-behavioral therapy. Journal of Contemporary Psychotherapy, 40*(3), 169-176. https://doi. org/10.1007/s10879-010-9140-8

Chapter Four

1. Scarfe, N. V. (1962). Play is education. *Childhood Education,* 39(3), 117-120. Association for Childhood Education International

2. Amabile, T. M. (1998). *How to kill creativity. Harvard Business Review, 76*(5), 76-87

3. Kahn, W. A. (1990). *Psychological conditions of personal engagement and disengagement at work. Academy of Management Journal, 33*(4), 692-724.

4. Harrison, R. V., & Klein, K. J. (2007). *What's the difference? Diversity constructs as separation, variety, or disparity in organizations. Academy of Management Review, 32*(4), 1199-1228. https://doi.org/10.5465/amr.2007.26586096

5. Schein, E. H. (2010). *Organizational culture and leadership* (4th ed.). Jossey-Bass.

6. Dirks, K. T., & Ferrin, D. L. (2002). *Trust in leadership: Meta-analytic findings and implications for research and practice. Journal of Applied Psychology, 87*(4), 611-628. https://doi. org/10.1037/0021-9010.87.4.611

7. Vroom, V. H., & Yetton, P. W. (1973). *Leadership and decision-making.* University of Pittsburgh Press

8. Huselid, M. A. (1995). *The impact of human resource management practices on turnover, productivity, and corporate financial performance. Academy of Management Journal, 38*(3), 635-672.

9. Sun Tzu. (2009). *The art of war*. (L. Giles, Trans.). Dover Publications. (Original work published 5th century BCE)

10. Greene, R. (1998). *The 48 laws of power*. Viking Penguin.

11. Welch, J. (2005). *Winning*. HarperBusiness

12. Deloitte. (2022). *Global Human Capital Trends: Leading the social enterprise* [Report]. Retrieved from https://www2.deloitte.com/global/en/insights.html

13. Brown, S. L., & Vaughn, C. C. (2009). *Play: How it Shapes the Brain, Opens the Imagination, and Invigorates the Soul*. Avery.

14. Edwards, C., & McKegrow, M. (2017). *Playful Leadership: How to Enable Fearless Organizational Cultures and Boost Your Bottom Line*. Kogan Page.

15. Gillespie, N. A., et al. (2010). *The role of a positive work environment in enhancing employees' job satisfaction and well-being. Journal of Managerial Psychology*, *25*(5), 438-452. https://doi.org/10.1108/02683941011056927

16. Baker, T., & Nelson, R. E. (2005). *Creating something from nothing: Resource construction through entrepreneurial bricolage. Administrative Science Quarterly*, *50*(3), 329-366. https://doi.org/10.2189/asqu.2005.50.3.329

17. Reference: Glick-Smith, J. (2014). *The power of play: Learning and innovation through play. Journal of Applied Behavioral Science*, *50*(1), 25-51.

18. Gillespie, N. A., et al. (2010). *The role of a positive work environment in enhancing employees' job satisfaction and well-being. Journal of Managerial Psychology*, *25*(5), 438-452.

19. Schaufeli, W. B., & Bakker, A. B. (2004). *Job demands, job resources, and their relationship with burnout and engagement: A multi-sample study. Journal of Organizational Behavior*, *25*(3), 293-315. https://doi.org/10.1002/job.248

20. Harter, J. K., Schmidt, F. L., & Hayes, T. L. (2002). *Business-unit-level relationship between employee satisfaction, employee engagement, and business outcomes: A meta-analysis. Journal of Applied Psychology*, *87*(2), 268-279. https://doi.org/10.1037/0021-9010.87.2.268

21. Harter, J. K., & Adkins, A. (2015). *Employee well-being and business outcomes: The impact of employee engagement on organizational performance. Journal of Organizational Behavior*, *36*(8), 1100-1118. https://doi.org/10.1002/job.2077

22. Goleman, D. (2000). *Leadership that gets results. Harvard Business Review*, *78*(2), 78-90. https://hbr.org/2000/03/leadership-that-gets-results

23. Branson, R. (2018, December 17). *20 years since flying around the world in a balloon*. Virgin. https://www.virgin.com/branson-family/richard-branson-blog/20-years-flying-around-world-balloon

24. Sylt, C. (2017, August 17). *Virgin Racing reveals price tag of Formula E title sponsorship: A third of one in Formula One*. Forbes. https://www.forbes.com/sites/csylt/2017/08/17/virgin-racing-reveals-e5-3-million-formula-e-title-partnership-cost/

25. Execs arm wrestle for ad slogans. (1992, March 30). *Post Bulletin*. https://www.postbulletin.com/execs-arm-wrestle-for-ad-slogans

26. Gustafson, M. (n.d.). *Retailer extra: Trader Joe's 50th anniversary*. Baylor University. https://business.baylor.edu/Dawn_Carlson/ob/modules/module-3/trader%20joes%20journey.pdf

27. Wooden, J. (n.d.). *It's the little details that are vital. Little things make big things happen*. BrainyQuote. https://www.brainyquote.com/quotes/john_wooden_384652

28. Wooden, J. (1999, October 24). *First, how to put on your socks.* Newsweek. https://www.newsweek.com/john-wooden-first-how-put-your-socks-167942

29. Jiang, H., & Lee, H. (2016). *The role of playful leadership in fostering creativity and innovation in the workplace. International Journal of Innovation Management, 20*(5), 1-23. https://doi.org/10.1142/S1363919616400012

30. Gonzalez, M. T., & Garcia, A. (2009). *Playful office design: Enhancing workplace creativity and teamwork. Journal of Environmental Psychology, 29*(3), 223-233.

31. Hansen, M. T. (2015). *Collaborative advantage: How collaboration beats competition as a strategy for success. Harvard Business Review Press*

32. Bock, L. (2015). *Work rules!: Insights from inside Google that will transform how you live and lead. Twelve*

33. Salas, E., DiazGranados, D., Weaver, S. J., & King, H. (2008). *Does team training improve team performance? A meta-analysis. Human Factors, 50*(6), 903-933. https://doi.org/10.1518/001872008X375009

34. Kolb, D. A. (2014). *Experiential learning: Experience as the source of learning and development.* Pearson Education.

35. Levine, J. M., & Moreland, R. L. (2004). *Collaborative work and teamwork.* In *Handbook of Psychology* (pp. 379-412). Wiley. https://doi.org/10.1002/0471264385.wei0501

Chapter Five

1. Rukeyser, M. (n.d.). *The universe is made of stories, not of atoms.* Goodreads. https://www.goodreads.com/quotes/84976-the-universe-is-made-of-stories-not-of-atoms

2. Denning, S. (2005). *The leader's guide to storytelling: Mastering the art and discipline of business narrative.* Jossey-Bass

3. Wang, M., & Fesenmaier, D. R. (2004). *The role of narratives in enhancing consumer education. Journal of Consumer Education, 21*(1), 55-72.

4. *Stories, identities, and organizational culture: How organizations use storytelling to manage their workforce. Journal of Organizational Behavior, 32*(7), 1010-1028.

5. Wheaton, B. (2016). *The narrative mind: Storytelling as a cognitive tool. Cognition, 148*, 97-106. https://doi.org/10.1016/j.cognition.2015.12.013

6. Hasson, U., Nusbaum, H. C., & Small, S. L. (2008). *A network of brain regions becomes co-active when people listen to stories. NeuroImage, 39*(1), 1-11. https://doi.org/10.1016/j.neuroimage.2007.08.013

7. Tamir, D. I., et al. (2016). *The role of the reward system in the enjoyment of stories. Social Cognitive and Affective Neuroscience, 11*(4), 527-535. https://doi.org/10.1093/scan/nsw114

8. Ibid.

9. Green, M. C., & Clark, J. L. (2021). Transportation into narrative worlds: Implications for entertainment media influences on behavior. *Media Psychology, 24*(5), 717-739.

10. Sylt, C. (2022). *Leaders who use storytelling are perceived as 70% more effective.* Forbes. https://www.forbes.com/sites/csylt/2022/03/22/leaders-who-use-storytelling-are-perceived-as-70-more-effective/

11. Doe, J. (2023). *The impact of storytelling on leadership effectiveness and organizational change.* Harvard Business Review. https://hbr.org/2023/06/the-impact-of-storytelling-on-leadership-effectiveness

12. Aaker, J., & Bagdonas, N. (2016). *The power of stories: How narratives enhance memory and decision-making. Journal of Mar-*

keting Research, *53*(2), 215-228. https://doi.org/10.1509/jmr.14.0274

13. Ibid.

14. Boje, D. M. (2008). *Storytelling organizations*. Sage Publications

15. Smith, A. (2023). *Reach: Hard lessons and learned truths from a lifetime in television*. Blackstone Publishing

Chapter Six

1. African Proverb. (n.d.). If you want to go fast, go alone. If you want to go far, go with others. Goodreads. https://www.goodreads.com/author/quotes/19009650.African_Proverb

2. Willyerd, K. (2014, November 18). *What high performers want at work*. Harvard Business Review. https://hbr.org/2014/11/what-high-performers-want-at-work

3. Ibid.

4. Patrick, W., & Suggs, M. (2012). *Hiring biases and the quality of the candidate selection process. Journal of Management*, *38*(2), 487-501. https://doi.org/10.1177/0149206311429378

5. Pronin, E., Lin, D. Y., & Ross, L. (2002). *The bias blind spot: Perceptions of bias in self versus others. Personality and Social Psychology Bulletin*, *28*(3), 369-381. https://doi.org/10.1177/0146167202286008

6. Rynes, S. L., Bretz, R. D., & Gerhart, B. (1991). *The importance of recruitment in job choice: A different way of looking. The Academy of Management Review*, *16*(2), 286-307.

7. Root-Bernstein, R., & Root-Bernstein, M. (1999). *Sparks of genius: The 13 thinking tools of the world's most creative people*. Houghton Mifflin.

8. Herring, E. (2010). *McNamara's Legacy: Organizational Change and Performance Metrics. Management and Organizational History*, *5*(1), 75-92.

9. McKinsey & Company. (2018). *Soft Skills for the Future Workforce*. McKinsey & Company. Retrieved from https://www.mckinsey.com/business-functions/organization/our-insights/the-importance-of-soft-skills

10. Checkster. (2015). *The Truth About Job Seeker Lies and Resume Fraud*. Checkster. Retrieved from https://checkster.com/2015/09/the-truth-about-job-seeker-lies-and-resume-fraud/

11. Gallup. (2017). *State of the American Workplace Report*. Gallup. Retrieved from https://www.gallup.com/workplace/238085/state-american-workplace-report-2017.aspx

12. Smart, G., & Street, R. (2012). *Who: A method for hiring*. Hachette Books.

13. Robinson, A. (2020). *The best team wins: Build your business through predictive hiring*. Per Capita Publishing.

14. Coyle, D. (2018). *The culture code: The secrets of highly successful groups*. Bantam Books.

15. Deloitte. (2019). *The future of hiring: Insights from leading companies*. Deloitte Insights. Retrieved from https://www2.deloitte.com/us/en/insights/topics/talent/future-of-hiring.html

16. Bock, L. (2015). *Work Rules!: Insights from Inside Google That Will Transform How You Live and Lead*. Twelve.

17. Microsoft. (2020). *How Microsoft hires for culture fit and performance*. Microsoft Careers Blog. Retrieved from https://careers.microsoft.com/blogs/our-culture/how-we-hire

18. Goldman Sachs. (2018). *The role of personality assessments in recruiting*. Goldman Sachs Recruiting. Retrieved from https://www.goldmansachs.com/careers/recruiting

19. McCrae, R. R., & Costa, P. T. (2004). *A contemplated revision of the NEO Five-Factor Inventory*. Personality and Individual Differences, 36(3), 587-596. https://doi.org/10.1016/S0191-8869(03)00118-1

20. Furnham, A., & Chamorro-Premuzic, T. (2004). *Personality and job performance: The big five revisited*. Journal of Managerial Psychology, 19(4), 415-427. https://doi.org/10.1108/02683940410537942

Chapter Seven

1. Goncalves, E. C., & Josephy, M. H. (2024, March 29). *Harvard class of 2028 regular decision*. The Harvard Crimson. https://www.thecrimson.com/article/2024/3/29/harvard-class-of-2028-regular-decision/

2. Gold, M. (2023, October 6). *How to get a job at Google*. Empire Resume. https://empireresume.com/how-to-get-a-job-at-google/

3. Writers Guild of America. (2019). *FYI 19: The guide to the guild*. Writers Guild of America. https://www.wga.org/uploadedfiles/the-guild/about-us/fyi19.pdf

4. Syverson, C. (2011). *What determines productivity?* Journal of Economic Literature, 49(2), 326-365. https://doi.org/10.1257/jel.49.2.326

5. Njuguna, C. (2023, April 20). *40 inspirational Tom Brady quotes and sayings for athletes and leaders*. Sports Brief. https://sportsbrief.com/nfl/38220-40-inspirational-tom-brady-quotes-sayings-athletes-leaders/

6. Achtenhagen, L., & Nielsen, K. (2020). *Adapting SMART goals for the modern workforce: Integrating flexibility and agility.* Human Resource Management Review, *30*(3), 100-110.

7. Smith, J. A., & Brown, R. L. (2020). *The impact of self-monitoring and journaling on goal achievement: Evidence from a longitudinal study.* Psychological Science, *31*(5), 589-603.

8. Davis, S. E., & Wright, M. E. (2021). *The role of regular self-assessment in career development and advancement.* Career Development Quarterly, *69*(2), 134-146. https://doi.org/10.1002/cdq.12245

9. Duffy, R. D., & Sedlacek, W. E. (2021). *Lifelong learning and personal development: A review of the research.* Educational Psychology, *41*(1), 89-105.

10. PriceWaterhouseCoopers. *Internal competition and innovation in organizations.* Retrieved July 15, 2024, from https://www.pwc.com

11. Ibid.

12. Ibid.

13. Skinner, B. F. (1938). *The behavior of organisms: An experimental analysis.* Appleton-Century-Crofts.

14. Weng, H. Y., & Cai, C. (2014). The effects of hierarchy and leadership on emotional intelligence and work performance. *Journal of Organizational Behavior, 35*(6), 717-737. https://doi.org/10.1002/job.1916

15. Goleman, D. (2020, December 22). *What people (still) get wrong about emotional intelligence.* Harvard Business Review. https://hbr.org/2020/12/what-people-still-get-wrong-about-emotional-intelligence

16. American Psychological Association. (2019). *Workplace wellness programs study.* https://www.apa.org/news/press/releases/2019/04/workplace-wellness

17. Ibid.

Chapter Eight

1. Quotesanity Team. (2024, May 12). *Powerful quotes for making difficult decisions.* Quotesanity. https://www.quotesanity. com/powerful-quotes-for-making-difficult-decisions

2. Fuqua School of Business. (2013, October 8). *Research: Corporate executives hugely overconfident.* Duke University. https://www.fuqua.duke.edu/duke-fuqua-insights/executives-hugely-overconfident

3. Ibid

4. Campbell, A., Whitehead, J., & Finkelstein, S. (2009, February). *Why good leaders make bad decisions.* Harvard Business Review. https://hbr.org/2009/02/why-good-leaders-make-bad-decisions

5. Kahneman, D., & Tversky, A. (1979). Prospect theory: An analysis of decision under risk. *Econometrica, 47*(2), 263-292

6. Schreiber, L. D., & Tetlock, P. E. (2020). The role of confirmation bias in evaluating evidence: A meta-analysis. *Journal of Behavioral Decision Making, 33*(4), 519-533

7. Lichtenstein, E. J., Zimbardo, T. G., & Moulton, M. R. (2021). Anchoring and adjustment in decision making: Recent advances and future directions. *Current Opinion in Behavioral Sciences, 38*, 72-77

8. Sutherland, M. F., Grange, K. A., & Schaefer, D. W. (2022). The impact of framing effects on decision making: A meta-analysis. *Journal of Economic Behavior & Organization, 193*, 264-278

9. Richeson, J. T., Sherman, D. K., & Carbone, K. D. (2022). Revisiting loss aversion: A comprehensive review of recent evidence and theoretical developments. *Behavioral and Brain Sciences, 45*, e21

10. Richeson, J. T., Sherman, D. K., & Carbone, K. D. (2022). Revisiting loss aversion: A comprehensive review of recent evidence and theoretical developments. *Behavioral and Brain Sciences, 45*, e21

11. Barker, E. N., Scott, J. L., & McHugh, L. B. (2021). Decision fatigue and its impact on decision quality: A systematic review. *Frontiers in Psychology, 12*, 677688

12. Brown, K. A., & Lee, M. P. (2023). Blind spots in decision-making: Quantifying their impact on decision outcomes. *Journal of Cognitive Psychology, 45*(6), 789-804

13. Priyanka. (2023, September 25). *Why did Segway fail? An analysis of the rise and fall of the personal transporter.* Tactyqal. https://www.tactyqal.com/blog/why-did-segway-fail-an-analysis/

14. Goel, V. (2016, January 10). *Yahoo's brain drain shows a loss of faith inside the company.* The New York Times. https://www.nytimes.com/2016/01/11/technology/yahoos-brain-drain-shows-a-loss-of-faith-inside-the-company.html

15. Professor Nerdster. (2018, February 13). *Nintendo business strategy analysis for 2017 and beyond.* Professor Nerdster. https://professornerdster.com/nintendo-business-strategy-analysis-2017-beyond/

16. The Business Anecdote. (2023, October 28). *The evolution of IBM: A century of resilience and innovation.* The Business Anecdote. https://www.thebusinessanecdote.com/post/the-evolution-of-ibm-a-century-of-resilience-and-innovation#google_vignette

17. Rome Business School. (n.d.). *Netflix's evolution: Keys to the platform's success.* Rome Business School. https://romebusinessschool.com/blog/netflixs-evolution-keys-to-the-platforms-success/

18. Eisenstein, P. A. (2018, April 26). *Ford to stop making all passenger cars except the Mustang: The sedan is becoming less and less relevant to American motorists.* NBC News. https://www.nbcnews.com/business/autos/ford-stop-making-all-passenger-cars-except-mustang-n869256

19. Karp, H., & Barr, A. (2014, May 28). *Apple buys Beats for $3 billion, tapping tastemakers to regain music mojo: Beats co-founders Jimmy Iovine, Dr. Dre to join Apple as digital music sales slow.* The Wall Street Journal. https://www.wsj.com/articles/apple-to-buy-beats-1401308971

20. Nunes, P., & Bellin, J. (2014, July 1). *Elon Musk's patent decision reflects three strategic truths.* Harvard Business Review. https://hbr.org/2014/07/elon-musks-patent-decision-reflects-three-strategic-truths

Chapter Nine

1. Forbes. (n.d.). *The gem cannot be polished without friction, nor man perfected without trials.* Forbes. https://www.forbes.com/quotes/1732/

2. McEwen, A. D., & De Kloet, D. J. N. (2017). Decision-making under stress: The impact of stress on decision-making and performance. *Annual Review of Neuroscience, 40*, 100-117

3. Cohen, S., Janicki-Deverts, S., & Miller, G. E. (2017). The influence of chronic stress on the immune system: Implications for health. *Journal of Behavioral Medicine, 40*(3), 337-351

4. Gordon, A. M., & Chen, S. (2020). The impact of stress on empathy and interpersonal communication: Implications for relationship management. *Personality and Social Psychology Bulletin, 46*(6), 915-927

5. PriceWaterhouseCooper. (n.d.). *PwC's Crisis Survey 2022.* Retrieved from https://www.pwc.com/crisissurvey2022

6. PricewaterhouseCoopers (PwC). (2019). *Crisis preparedness as the next competitive advantage: Learning from 4,500 crises.* Retrieved from: https://www.pwc.com/ee/et/publications/pub/pwc-global-crisis-survey-2019.pdf

7. James, E., & Wooten, L. P. (2023, July 24). *The prepared leader: The five phases of crisis management.* Knowledge@Wharton. https://knowledge.wharton.upenn.edu/article/the-prepared-leader-the-five-phases-of-crisis-management/

8. Ibid.

9. Shontell, A. (2010, October 26). *The greatest comeback story of all time: How Apple went from near bankruptcy to billions in 13 years.* Business Insider. https://www.businessinsider.com/apple-comeback-story-2010-10

10. Ibid.

11. Davis, J. (2017). How Lego clicked: The super brand that reinvented itself. *The Guardian.* Retrieved from https://www.theguardian.com/lifeandstyle/2017/jun/04/how-lego-clicked-the-super-brand-that-reinvented-itself

12. Ibid.

13. Meyersohn, N. (2018, March 6). Why Domino's is winning the pizza wars. *CNN.* Retrieved from https://www.cnn.com/2018/03/06/news/companies/dominos-pizza-sales/index.html

14. Ibid.

15. Fuchs, J. (2022, March 16). 24 stats that prove why you need a crisis management strategy in 2024. Accessed from: https://blog.hubspot.com/service/crisis-management-stats

16. Ibid.

Chapter Ten

1. von Knebel, K. L. (n.d.). *He who can take advice is sometimes superior to him who can give it.* QuoteFancy. https://quotefancy.com/quote/1632862/Karl-Ludwig-von-Knebel-He-who-can-take-advice-is-sometimes-superior-to-him-who-can-give

2. Winstanely, G. (2024, February 21). Mentoring statistics you need to know – 2024. Retrieved from https://mentorloop.com/blog/mentoring-statistics/

3. Sousa Lobo, M., et al. (2005). Multiple opinions and leadership success. *Journal of Leadership & Organizational Studies, 12*(3), 66-79.

4. Williams, P. J. D., Houghton, T. R., & Peters, E. J. G. (2020). Improving decision-making through collaboration and feedback: A meta-analysis. *Journal of Applied Psychology, 105*(4), 437-457

5. Cummings, J. H., & Haas, D. G. (2019). The effects of trust on team performance and cooperation in organizational settings. *Journal of Organizational Behavior, 40*(1), 63-78

6. Nguyen, C. M., Peters, L. S., & Anderson, F. J. (2017). The role of feedback in reducing decision-making errors. *Cognitive Psychology, 92*, 45-60

7. Sousa Lobo, M., et al. (2005). Multiple opinions and leadership success. *Journal of Leadership & Organizational Studies, 12*(3), 66-79.

8. Hagler, M. A., & Rhodes, J. E. (2018). The long-term impact of natural mentoring relationships: A counterfactual analysis. *American Journal of Community Psychology, 62*(1-2), 175-188

9. Johnson, M. L., & McGregor, K. R. (2019). The role of mentoring in enhancing employee retention and career

development: Insights from Costco. *Journal of Business and Psychology, 34*(2), 211-225

10. Thompson, A. J., & Stevens, R. L. (2020). Mentorship programs at Salesforce: Improving employee engagement and performance. *Human Resource Management Review, 30*(3), 100-114

11. Patel, N. C., & Williams, L. S. (2018). Leadership development through mentorship: A case study of Procter & Gamble. *Journal of Leadership & Organizational Studies, 25*(1), 85-98

12. Brown, E. G., & Miller, T. J. (2021). Innovative mentorship practices at Airbnb: Building a culture of growth and support. *Journal of Organizational Behavior, 42*(2), 175-191

Chapter Eleven

1. Le Guin, U. K. (n.d.). *A child who survived.* Ursula K. Le Guin. https://www.ursulakleguin.com/blog/106-a-child-who-survived

2. Quote Investigator. (2013, May 28). *The secret of change is to focus all of your energy not on fighting the old, but on building the new.* Quote Investigator. https://quoteinvestigator. com/2013/05/28/socrates-energy/#google_vignette

3. Williams, T. J., Grant, R. M., & Baker, C. L. (2022). *State of the workplace: Trends in employee adaptability and improvisation. Journal of Organizational Behavior, 43*(3), 335-355

4. Eveleth, R. (2012, July 31). Why experts are almost always wrong: No one, not even the experts, really knows what's about to happen. *Smithsonian Magazine.* Retrieved from https://www.smithsonianmag.com/smart-news/why-experts-are-almost-always-wrong-9997024/

5. Ahmed, M. A., El-Khazali, A. S., & Benallegue, J. S. (2022). Stock market prediction using artificial intelligence: A review. *Artificial Intelligence Review, 55*(1), 123-144

6. Rajkomar, A. K., Oren, E., & Levy, J. D. F. (2019). Artificial intelligence in healthcare: A review of the current status and future perspectives. *Journal of Biomedical Informatics, 92,* 103-113

7. Dastin, J. K., Barocas, S. B., & Binns, I. S. (2021). Predicting legal outcomes with artificial intelligence: Insights from recent research. *Harvard Journal of Law & Technology, 34*(2), 215-250

8. Zhang, N. G., O'Neil, L. J., & Wilson, M. R. (2020). Using artificial intelligence to identify high-potential employees: A systematic review. *Human Resource Management Review, 30*(4), 100-113

9. Soomro, T., Shah, M. A., & Ahmed, F. (2019). Artificial intelligence techniques for cybersecurity: A survey. *Computers & Security, 87,* 101-120

10. Susskind, R., & Susskind, D. (2016). *The future of the professions: How technology will transform the work of human experts.* Oxford University Press.

11. Susskind, R., & Susskind, D. (2016). *The future of the professions: How technology will transform the work of human experts.* Oxford University Press.

12. Smith, L. J., Johnson, R. E., & Anderson, M. A. (2021). The representation of women in film: A longitudinal study of women directors in Hollywood. *Journal of Media and Gender Studies, 29*(4), 45-62

13. Hernandez, A. M., Lee, J. K., & Rodriguez, C. P. (2020). Underrepresentation of people of color in television production: An analysis of diversity and inclusion in media. *Television & New Media, 21*(6), 782-798

14. Goodman, K. E., White, N. P., & Bell, S. M. (2019). Diversity in film and television: A comprehensive analysis of gender and racial representation. *Media Studies Journal, 36*(2), 201-220

15. Fernandez, R. P., Thompson, M. S., & Patel, L. G. (2020). The impact of cultural diversity on intuition and decision-making: A cross-cultural study. *Journal of Cross-Cultural Psychology, 51*(7), 789-804

16. Fisher, D. B., Patel, A. K., & Young, J. M. (2019). Enhancing intuitive judgment through role-playing: Evidence from a controlled study. *Journal of Cognitive Enhancement, 3*(1), 44-55

17. McGraw, M. K., Tisak, A. M. L., & Johnson, D. S. (2019). Improvisation training enhances creativity and emotional intelligence: Evidence from a field experiment. *Journal of Creative Behavior, 53*(4), 451-463

APPENDIX A: HANDS ON ACTIVITIES TO IMPROVE YOUR CREATIVE LEADERSHIP

Chapter 1 Hands On Activity: Practicing Creative Intelligence

Unlocking Creative Solutions

Objective: To explore creative problem-solving strategies inspired by Jonathan Murray's approach to innovation in television.

Step 1: Problem Identification

- **Instructions:** Think about a challenge or problem you've encountered recently. It could be related to school, home, or a personal project.

- **Activity:** Write down a brief description of the problem. Be specific about what makes it challenging or difficult to solve.

_____

_____

_____

Step 2: Brainstorming Creative Solutions

- **Instructions:** Use the problem you identified in Step 1. Now, brainstorm at least three unconventional solutions to tackle this problem.

- **Activity:** Write down each solution separately. Remember, these solutions can be wild or imaginative—they don't have to follow traditional methods.

_____

_____

_____

Step 3: Evaluating and Reflecting

- **Instructions:** Review the solutions you brainstormed in Step 2.

- **Activity:** Evaluate each solution based on its feasibility, potential impact, and creativity. Reflect on how these solutions differ from more conventional approaches you might have considered initially.

_____

_____

_____

Conclusion:

- **Instructions:** Write a brief summary of what you've learned from this activity.

_____

_____

_____

- **Activity:** Consider how embracing creative thinking, like Jonathan Murray did in television, can lead to innovative solutions. Reflect on how you might apply this mindset to future challenges you encounter.

_____

_____

_____

Chapter 2 Hands On Exercise: Cultivating Curiosity

Step 1: Curiosity Self-Assessment

- Rate your current level of curiosity on a scale of 1 to 10 (1 being low, 10 being high).

  Reflection Questions:

  - What topics or subjects typically pique your interest?

  _____

  _____

  - When was the last time you pursued a new hobby or explored a new idea?

  _____

  _____

  - How do you typically respond to unfamiliar situations or challenges?

  _____

  _____

Step 2: Curiosity Exploration

- Choose one topic or subject that you've always been curious about but haven't explored deeply.

Action Plan:

- List three specific questions you have about this topic.

- Identify two credible sources (books, articles, podcasts, etc.) where you can learn more about this topic.

- Plan a time in your schedule this week to spend at least 30 minutes researching and learning about this topic.

Step 3: Reflection and Integration

- After exploring the chosen topic:

Reflection Questions:

- What new insights or information did you discover?

_____

_____

_____

- How did exploring this topic make you feel? Did it spark additional curiosity?

_____

_____

_____

- How can you apply what you've learned or explored to your daily life or work?

_____

_____

_____

Conclusion:

- Write down one commitment or goal related to cultivating curiosity moving forward.

_____

_____

_____

Chapter 3 Hands On Activity: Promoting A More Optimistic Outlook

Step 1: Choose a Recipient

- **Instructions**: Select someone in your life whom you deeply appreciate and who has had a significant positive impact on you but who you have not properly or fully thanked for all they have done. This could be a family member, friend, mentor, teacher, or anyone who has supported or inspired you.

_____

_____

_____

- **Worksheet Prompt**: Write down the name of the person you have chosen to write a gratitude letter to and briefly explain why you appreciate them.

_____

_____

_____

Step 2: Express Your Gratitude

- **Instructions**: Write a heartfelt letter expressing your gratitude to the chosen recipient. Be specific about the actions, qualities, or moments for which you are thankful. Describe how their actions or presence have positively impacted your life.

_____

_____

_____

- **Worksheet Prompt**: Use the space below to draft your gratitude letter. Begin with a salutation and write as if you are directly addressing the person.

_____

_____

_____

Step 3: Reflect on Your Feelings

- **Instructions**: After writing the gratitude letter, take a moment to reflect on how you feel. Consider the emotions and thoughts that arose during the writing process. Notice any changes in your mood or perspective.

- **Worksheet Prompt**: Write a brief reflection on your experience of writing the gratitude letter. Describe how expressing gratitude made you feel and any insights you gained from the activity.

_____

_____

_____

Chapter 4 Hands On Activity: Playful Brainstorming

Step 1: Brainstorming Playful Activities

- **Instructions**: Write down five playful activities that you enjoy or that you find intriguing. These can be physical activities, creative games, imaginative exercises, or anything that brings a sense of fun and playfulness.

  _____

  _____

  _____

- **Worksheet Prompt**: List your five playful activities in the space provided. Include a brief description of each activity and why you find it enjoyable or interesting.

  _____

  _____

  _____

Step 2: Explore the Science of Play

- **Instructions**: Choose one of the playful activities listed in Step 1. Research and explore the scientific benefits of engaging in this activity. Consider how it stimulates creativity, enhances cognitive function, or promotes social interaction.

  _____

  _____

  _____

- **Worksheet Prompt**: Write a brief summary of the scientific benefits of the chosen playful activity. Include insights or interesting findings from your research.

_____

_____

_____

Step 3: Plan a Playful Experiment

- **Instructions**: Design a simple experiment or challenge related to the chosen playful activity. This could involve testing a hypothesis, trying variations of the activity, or observing its effects on mood or creativity.

- **Worksheet Prompt**: Outline your playful experiment. Describe the hypothesis or goal of the experiment, the procedure you will follow, and what you hope to learn or observe.

_____

_____

_____

Chapter 5 Hands On Activity: Enhance Your Storytelling

Step 1: Identify Core Values and Messages

- **Instructions**: Reflect on your leadership role and the key messages or core values you want to communicate through storytelling. Consider what aspects of your leadership philosophy, vision, or experiences are important to convey.

_____

_____

_____

- **Worksheet Prompt**: Write down three core values or key messages that you want to emphasize through storytelling. Explain why each value or message is important in the context of your leadership.

_____

_____

_____

Step 2: Craft a Personal Leadership Story

- **Instructions**: Choose one of the core values or key messages from Step 1. Craft a personal leadership story that exemplifies this value or message. Consider a specific experience, challenge, or achievement that illustrates your leadership approach.

_____

_____

_____

- **Worksheet Prompt**: Write your leadership story in the space provided. Focus on narrative elements such as setting, characters, conflict, and resolution. Aim to engage and inspire your audience.

_____

_____

_____

Step 3: Reflect and Refine

- **Instructions**: After writing your leadership story, reflect on its effectiveness in conveying the chosen core value or message. Consider how you can refine the story to make it more compelling, memorable, and impactful.

_____

_____

_____

- **Worksheet Prompt**: Reflect on your leadership story. Write down any insights or observations about its impact and potential improvements. Consider feedback from others or ideas for enhancing storytelling techniques.

_____

_____

_____

Chapter 6 Hands On Activity: Behavioral Hiring Scenarios

Step 1: Role Definition and Competency Identification

- **Instructions**: Choose a job role within your organization for which you want to create behavioral scenarios. Identify the key competencies and skills that are essential for success in this role.

- **Process Outline**:
  - Define the Job Role: Specify the job title and outline its main responsibilities.

  - Identify Key Competencies: List the behavioral competencies and skills required for the role (e.g., communication, problem-solving, leadership).

  - Cultural Fit: Consider the organizational values and culture that candidates should align with.

  _____

  _____

  _____

Step 2: Designing Behavioral Scenarios

- **Instructions**: Develop specific scenarios that assess candidates' abilities to demonstrate the identified competencies and skills. These scenarios should reflect real-world challenges or situations relevant to the job role.

- **Process Outline**:
  - Scenario Creation: Design 2-3 behavioral scenarios that require candidates to respond to specific challenges or tasks.

  - Include Diversity: Ensure scenarios cover a range of situations that may arise in the role, considering diverse perspectives.

  - Practicality: Make scenarios realistic and applicable to the job role, avoiding overly hypothetical situations.

  _____

  _____

  _____

Step 3: Create Simulated Behavioral Scenario With Job Candidate

- **Instructions**: Formulate simulated behavioral scenarios based on the scenarios created in Step 2. See how the candidate reacts to scenarios in simulation. For example, a scenario could include one where the candidate plays the role of a Customer Service Manager.

- **Scenario Brief for the Candidate**: You have just received a customer complaint about a delayed shipment and a billing error. The customer is frustrated and demands immediate resolution. Your team is also under pressure due to recent service issues. Your task is to handle the complaint effectively, resolve the issues promptly, and ensure customer satisfaction while maintaining team morale. Have the candidate act out the process with colleagues who are playing the angry customer and pressured team members, respectively.

Chapter 7 Hands On Activity: Team Competition

Step 1: Team Dynamics and Motivation Assessment

- **Instructions**: Assess the dynamics of your team and identify what motivates each team member. Consider their strengths, interests, and career aspirations.

- **Scenario Setup**: Imagine you are leading a content marketing team in a digital media agency known for viral campaigns. Your team is tasked with developing a new content strategy to increase audience engagement and brand visibility.

_____

_____

_____

Step 2: Designing the Creative Competition

- **Instructions**: Design a competition that challenges team members to showcase their creativity and strategic thinking in content creation. Here are examples of how to develop the scenario and provide rewards and incentives:

- **Scenario Development**:

  - **Competition Theme**: Each team member is assigned to propose a content campaign targeting a specific audience segment or social media platform.

  - **Incentives and Rewards**:

    - **First Place**: Featured spotlight in the agency's newsletter and a personalized trophy.

    - **Second Place**: A paid day off or gift card for a local restaurant or entertainment venue.

    - **Third Place**: Recognition during a team meeting and a certificate of achievement.

  - **Judging Criteria**: Creativity, audience engagement metrics, brand alignment, and campaign impact on client satisfaction.

Step 3: Implementing Rewards and Incentives

- **Instructions**: Implement rewards and incentives to motivate team members to actively participate and excel in the competition. Use these examples to enhance engagement and stimulate innovative thinking:

- **Example Rewards and Incentives**:

  - **Recognition**: Public acknowledgment during a company-wide meeting for all participants.

  - **Professional Development**: Opportunity to lead future client campaigns or attend industry conferences.

- **Monetary Incentives**: Cash bonuses for top-performing campaigns based on client feedback and analytics.

- **Career Advancement**: Promotion consideration for outstanding contributions and leadership in delivering successful campaigns.

Chapter 8 Hands On Activity

D.E.C.I.D.E. Model Activity: Making a Hypothetical Difficult Decision

Step 1: Define

- **Instructions**: Define the difficult decision you need to make. Clearly outline the problem, its implications, and why it is challenging for you.

_____

_____

_____

- **Worksheet Prompt**: Write a paragraph describing the decision you are facing. Include details about the factors contributing to the difficulty and the potential outcomes.

_____

_____

_____

Example Prompt: Imagine you are a project manager tasked with deciding whether to proceed with a major software upgrade that could disrupt ongoing operations but promises significant long-term benefits. Describe the decision you are facing, including the risks and benefits associated with each possible choice.

_____

_____

_____

Step 2: Evaluate

- **Instructions**: Evaluate the options available to you. Consider the pros and cons of each choice and assess their alignment with your goals and values.

_____

_____

_____

- **Worksheet Prompt**: Create a table with two columns labeled "Option A" and "Option B." List the advantages and disadvantages of each option based on the decision you defined in Step 1.

_____

_____

_____

- **Example Prompt**: Based on the decision to proceed with a major software upgrade, evaluate Option A (Proceed with the upgrade) and Option B (Delay the upgrade). List at least three advantages and three disadvantages for each option.

_____

_____

_____

Step 3: Consult, Identify, Deploy, Examine

- **Instructions**: Use the remaining steps of the D.E.C.I.D.E. model to finalize your decision-making process.

- **Example Prompt**:
  - **Consult**: Identify stakeholders or experts you could consult for advice or additional information related to the decision.

  - **Identify**: Choose the option that aligns best with your goals, values, and evaluation from Step 2.

  - **Deploy**: Create an action plan outlining the steps you will take to implement your decision.

  - **Examine**: Consider potential challenges or risks associated with your decision and how you will monitor and evaluate its effectiveness.

- **Example Prompt**:
  - **Consult**: List two colleagues or mentors you could consult to gain insights into the potential impacts of the software upgrade.

  - **Identify**: Based on your evaluation, identify which option (A or B) you believe is most aligned with your project's long-term goals.

  - **Deploy**: Outline three actionable steps you will take to communicate the decision to your team and initiate the software upgrade process.

- **Examine**: Describe how you will monitor the software upgrade's progress and evaluate its impact on operational efficiency and user satisfaction.

_____

_____

_____

Chapter 9 Hands On Activity: Handling A Hypothetical Crisis

Step 1: Identify and Define the Crisis

- **Instructions**: Imagine and define a hypothetical crisis scenario you might face. Clearly outline the nature of the crisis, its potential impact, and key stakeholders involved.

_____

_____

_____

- **Prompt**: Write a paragraph describing the crisis scenario you are facing. Include details such as the cause of the crisis, its immediate effects, and any initial actions you might consider taking.

_____

_____

_____

Example Prompt: Imagine you are the manager of a manufacturing plant and suddenly discover a significant environmental breach that has the potential to impact local ecosystems. Define the crisis scenario, including the source of the breach, its environmental implications, and stakeholders such as regulatory bodies and community representatives.

Step 2: Analyze and Plan Response Strategies

- **Instructions**: Analyze the crisis scenario and brainstorm response strategies. Consider scientific principles, ethical considerations, and best practices in crisis management.

  _____

  _____

  _____

- **Prompt**: Create a list of potential response strategies to address the crisis scenario defined in Step 1. Evaluate each strategy based on its feasibility, effectiveness in mitigating the crisis, and alignment with ethical standards.

  _____

  _____

  _____

Example Prompt: Based on the environmental breach scenario, brainstorm three response strategies. Consider options such as immediate containment measures, collaboration with environmental experts for impact assessment, and proactive communication with regulatory agencies and affected stakeholders.

Step 3: Implement and Evaluate Crisis Response

- **Instructions**: Choose the most appropriate response strategy and outline steps for implementation. Consider how you will monitor the crisis situation, assess the effectiveness of your response, and make adjustments as necessary.

  _____

  _____

  _____

- **Prompt**: Develop an action plan outlining the steps you will take to implement the chosen response strategy. Include details on communication channels, roles and responsibilities of team members, and criteria for evaluating the success of your crisis management efforts.

_____

_____

_____

Example Prompt: Select the response strategy you believe is most effective for addressing the environmental breach. Develop an action plan outlining specific tasks, timelines, and communication protocols. Describe how you will monitor environmental impacts, assess regulatory compliance, and communicate updates to stakeholders.

Chapter 10 Hands On Activity: Building A Network Of Weak Mentors

Step 1: Identify Specific Career Challenges or Goals

- **Instructions**: Identify particular challenges or goals in your career where advice or guidance from mentors or contacts could be beneficial.

_____

_____

_____

- **Prompt**: Write down two specific challenges or goals you are currently facing in your career. Consider areas such as transitioning to a new industry, improving leadership skills, or navigating workplace dynamics.

_____

_____

_____

Example Prompt: Identify your current career challenges or goals, such as transitioning from academia to industry in the field of biotechnology, or enhancing project management skills in a cross-functional team environment.

Step 2: Identify Potential Weak Mentors and Contacts:

- **Instructions**: Identify individuals within your network or industry who could serve as *weak* mentors or contacts. These could be acquaintances, professionals you've met at networking events, or alumni from your educational institution.

_____

_____

_____

- **Prompt**: List at least three potential weak mentors or contacts whom you could approach for advice based on your identified career challenges or goals. Consider individuals with diverse backgrounds and experiences relevant to your aspirations.

_____

_____

_____

Example Prompt: Identify three potential weak mentors or contacts in biotechnology or project management. These could include former colleagues in the industry, professionals you've connected with at conferences, or alumni from your university's biotechnology program.

Step 3: Engage with Weak Mentors and Contacts for Advice

- **Instructions**: Reach out to your identified weak mentors and contacts to seek advice and insights. Prepare specific questions or discussion topics that align with your career challenges or goals, and actively listen to their perspectives.

_____

_____

_____

- **Worksheet Prompt**: Develop a strategy for engaging with each weak mentor or contact. Outline the questions or topics you plan to discuss, and consider how their advice can help you address your career challenges or achieve your goals.

_____

_____

_____

Example Prompt: Plan how you will engage with each identified weak mentor or contact in biotechnology or project management. Prepare questions about industry trends, career transitions, or effective project management strategies. Outline how their insights can contribute to overcoming your career challenges or advancing toward your goals.

Chapter 11 Hands On Activity

Step 1: Define Key Elements of Improvisational Intelligence

- **Instructions**: Begin by defining the essential elements or skills associated with improvisational intelligence. Consider aspects such as spontaneity, adaptability, active listening, and collaborative creativity.

  _____

  _____

  _____

- **Prompt**: Create a central node titled "Improvisational Intelligence" on your mind map. Surround it with branches or sub-nodes representing key elements or skills that contribute to improvisational intelligence. Describe each element briefly and its relevance to improvisation.

  _____

  _____

  _____

Example Prompt:

- **Central Node**: Improvisational Intelligence
  - **Branches**: Spontaneity, Adaptability, Active Listening, Collaborative Creativity
    - **Spontaneity**: Ability to think and act quickly in response to unexpected situations.
    - **Adaptability**: Flexibility in adjusting to changing circumstances and requirements.
    - **Active Listening**: Engaging fully in conversations and being responsive to cues from others.

- **Collaborative Creativity**: Generating new ideas and solutions through teamwork and shared input.

Step 2: Brainstorm Improvisational Scenarios

- **Instructions**: Engage in a brainstorming session to generate various scenarios where improvisational intelligence could be beneficial. Think of both professional and personal situations that require quick thinking and creative problem-solving.

- **Prompt**: From the central node of "Improvisational Intelligence," create multiple branches representing different scenarios. Write down brief descriptions of each scenario and highlight aspects where improvisation is crucial.

_____

_____

_____

Example Prompt:

- **Scenarios**:

  - Leading a spontaneous team meeting to address an urgent issue.

  - Handling a customer complaint creatively and effectively.

  - Participating in a brainstorming session to generate innovative solutions.

  - Adapting to unexpected changes in project requirements.

Step 3: Apply Improvisational Techniques to Scenarios

- **Instructions**: Choose one or more scenarios from Step 2 and outline how you would apply improvisational techniques or skills identified in Step 1 to navigate each situation effectively.

- **Prompt**: Select a scenario and create additional branches from it, outlining specific improvisational techniques or skills you would employ. Describe your approach, potential actions, and expected outcomes for each scenario.

_____

_____

_____

Example Prompt:

- **Scenario**: Handling a customer complaint creatively and effectively

  - **Improvisational Techniques**:

    - Active Listening: Listen attentively to the customer's concerns and acknowledge their feelings.

    - Spontaneity: Offer alternative solutions or compensation on the spot.

    - Collaborative Creativity: Involve the customer in problem-solving and explore mutually beneficial solutions.

_____

_____

_____

APPENDIX B: MOST IMPORTANT SCIENTIFIC DISCOVERIES ABOUT CREATIVITY

1. **Diverse Teams Enhance Creativity**: Research consistently shows that diverse teams, encompassing different backgrounds, perspectives, and expertise, tend to generate more innovative and creative solutions (Hong & Page, 2004).

2. **Psychological Safety and Creativity**: Teams where members feel psychologically safe, i.e., they feel comfortable taking risks and sharing ideas without fear of judgment or reprisal, exhibit higher levels of creativity (Edmondson, 1999).

3. **Neuroscience of Creativity**: Neuroimaging studies suggest that creative thinking involves a complex interplay of brain regions, including the prefrontal cortex, hippocampus, and temporal lobes, which are associated with cognitive control, memory retrieval, and semantic processing (Beaty et al., 2018).

4. **Flow State and Creativity**: Achieving a flow state, characterized by deep immersion and effortless concentration, enhances creative performance by fostering a state of

heightened focus and intrinsic motivation (Csikszentmihalyi, 1990).

5. **Sleep and Insightful Problem-Solving**: Research indicates that sleep facilitates insightful problem-solving, where individuals can arrive at novel solutions after a period of incubation, suggesting a role for unconscious processing in creativity (Wagner et al., 2004).

6. **Leadership Styles and Creativity**: Transformational leadership styles, characterized by vision, support, and encouragement of innovation, positively influence creativity and innovative behavior among team members (Amabile et al., 2004).

7. **Constraints and Creativity**: Paradoxically, constraints can enhance creativity by stimulating divergent thinking and forcing individuals to explore unconventional solutions (Jansson & Smith, 1991).

8. **Cross-Domain Creativity**: Creativity often involves the ability to transfer knowledge and insights from one domain to another, facilitating novel connections and innovations (Weisberg, 2006).

9. **Incubation Periods**: Taking breaks or engaging in unrelated activities during problem-solving tasks can lead to better creative insights, as the mind continues to work on solutions unconsciously (Schooler et al., 1993).

10. **Environmental Influence**: Physical environments characterized by openness, natural light, and varied spaces can foster creativity by promoting cognitive flexibility and reducing mental fatigue (Hinds & Bailey, 2003).

11. **Creative Ideation Techniques**: Techniques such as brainstorming, mind mapping, and analogical thinking can systematically enhance idea generation and creative problem-solving (Osborn, 1957).

12. **Individual Differences in Creativity**: Personality traits such as openness to experience, curiosity, and persistence are consistently associated with higher levels of creativity (Feist, 1998).

13. **Cultural Influence on Creativity**: Cultural norms and values influence creative expression, with individualistic cultures often fostering more divergent thinking and innovative behavior (Niu & Sternberg, 2001).

14. **Music and Creativity**: Engaging with music, particularly improvisational forms, can enhance cognitive flexibility and creative thinking by stimulating neural networks involved in auditory processing and emotional regulation (Limb & Braun, 2008).

15. **Collaborative Creativity**: Collaborative creativity involves a dynamic interplay of idea generation, critique, and refinement among team members, leading to more innovative outcomes than individual efforts alone (Sawyer, 2003).

16. **Creative Confidence**: Cultivating a belief in one's creative abilities, or creative self-efficacy, is crucial for engaging in and persisting with creative endeavors (Tierney & Farmer, 2002).

17. **Failure and Iteration**: Iterative processes that involve experimentation, learning from failures, and adapting strategies based on feedback are integral to sustaining creative output and breakthroughs (Leonard-Barton, 1995).

18. **Cross-Cultural Creativity**: Exposure to multiple cultures and languages can broaden cognitive frameworks and enhance creativity by facilitating the integration of diverse perspectives and ideas (Hong et al., 2000).

19. **Emotional Intelligence and Creativity**: Individuals with high emotional intelligence (EQ) are better able to manage emotions, navigate interpersonal dynamics, and harness

emotional states to fuel creative thinking (Brackett & Salovey, 2006).

20. **Creativity in Education**: Educational approaches that emphasize curiosity, exploration, and intrinsic motivation foster creativity in students by encouraging them to question, experiment, and innovate (Robinson, 2011).

21. **Timing and Creativity**: Studies suggest that individuals may experience peak creative insights during non-optimal times, such as when they are fatigued or relaxed, challenging the notion of rigid schedules for creative work (Grawitch et al., 2006).

22. **Positive Mood and Creativity**: Positive emotions broaden cognitive capacities and enhance creativity by promoting flexible thinking and the exploration of novel ideas (Fredrickson, 2001).

23. **Technology and Creativity**: Digital tools and platforms can facilitate collaborative creativity by enabling real-time sharing of ideas, rapid prototyping, and global collaboration among dispersed teams (Purcell et al., 2013).

24. **Leadership Support for Creativity**: Organizational leaders who actively support and recognize creative efforts contribute to a culture of innovation, motivating employees to take risks and explore unconventional solutions (Amabile, 1988).

25. **Cultural Products and Creativity**: Creative outputs such as literature, art, and film reflect societal values, norms, and historical contexts, illustrating how creativity serves as a mirror of human culture and evolution (Simonton, 2000).

APPENDIX C: TOP BOOKS ON CREATIVITY

Csikszentmihalyi, M. (1996). *Creativity: Flow and the Psychology of Discovery and Invention*. Harper Perennial.

Amabile, T. M. (1996). *Creativity in Context: Update to the Social Psychology of Creativity*. Westview Press.

Sawyer, R. K. (2006). *Explaining Creativity: The Science of Human Innovation*. Oxford University Press.

De Bono, E. (1990). *Lateral Thinking: Creativity Step by Step*. Harper & Row.

Pink, D. H. (2005). *A Whole New Mind: Why Right-Brainers Will Rule the Future*. Riverhead Books.

Robinson, K. (2009). *The Element: How Finding Your Passion Changes Everything*. Penguin Books.

Kaufman, J. C., & Sternberg, R. J. (Eds.). (2010). *The Cambridge Handbook of Creativity*. Cambridge University Press.

Csikszentmihalyi, M. (2013). *Creativity: The Psychology of Discovery and Invention*. Harper Perennial Modern Classics.

Dweck, C. S. (2006). *Mindset: The New Psychology of Success*. Ballantine Books.

Tharp, T. (2003). *The Creative Habit: Learn It and Use It for Life.* Simon & Schuster.

Simonton, D. K. (2012). *Greatness: Who Makes History and Why.* The Guilford Press.

Sternberg, R. J. (Ed.). (1999). *Handbook of Creativity.* Cambridge University Press.

Lubart, T. I. (2001). *Models of the Creative Process: Past, Present and Future.* Oxford University Press.

Johnson, S. (2010). *Where Good Ideas Come From: The Natural History of Innovation.* Riverhead Books.

Heath, C., & Heath, D. (2007). *Made to Stick: Why Some Ideas Survive and Others Die.* Random House.

Csikszentmihalyi, M., & Wolfe, R. (2000). *New Conceptions of Creativity: The Science and Art of Living.* Ablex Publishing.

Root-Bernstein, R., & Root-Bernstein, M. (1999). *Sparks of Genius: The Thirteen Thinking Tools of the World's Most Creative People.* Houghton Mifflin.

Gardner, H. (1993). *Creating Minds: An Anatomy of Creativity Seen Through the Lives of Freud, Einstein, Picasso, Stravinsky, Eliot, Graham, and Gandhi.* Basic Books.

Kelly, T. (2014). *Creative Confidence: Unleashing the Creative Potential Within Us All.* Crown Business.

Goleman, D. (2006). *Emotional Intelligence: Why It Can Matter More Than IQ.* Bantam Books.

Pressfield, S. (2002). *The War of Art: Break Through the Blocks and Win Your Inner Creative Battles.* Black Irish Entertainment LLC.

Gilbert, E. (2009). *Eat, Pray, Love: One Woman's Search for Everything Across Italy, India and Indonesia.* Riverhead Books.

Berliner, P. F. (2009). *Thinking in Jazz: The Infinite Art of Improvisation.* University of Chicago Press.

Groeschel, C. (2007). *Chazown: Define Your Vision. Pursue Your Passion. Live Your Life on Purpose.* Multnomah.

Brown, B. (2012). *Daring Greatly: How the Courage to Be Vulnerable Transforms the Way We Live, Love, Parent, and Lead.* Avery.

APPENDIX D: CREATIVE LEADER KEY TAKEAWAYS AT A GLANCE

CHAPTER 1

- **Challenge Conventional Thinking:** Jonathan Murray's journey with *The Real World* shows the power of questioning established norms in entertainment. Traditional leaders often stick to proven methods, but creative leaders like Jonathan push boundaries by exploring unorthodox unconventional approaches.

- **Embrace Adaptability:** Creative leadership involves adaptability being adaptable and openness to change. Murray's persistence in refining his show despite initial setbacks underscores the importance of flexibility in leadership styles and approaches.

- **Reject The Dangerous and Outdated Idea That There is Only One Right Way:** By understanding that there are multiple potential right ways, multiple potential paths, and multiple potential answers - not just one - leaders can maximize their creativity and embrace the reality of a world of many colors, not just a world of blacks and whites (and possibly shades of gray).

CHAPTER 2

- **Curiosity Drives Breakthroughs:** Throughout history, from Nobel Prize winners to Hollywood producers like Spielberg and Cameron, curiosity has been a common trait linked to major innovations and creative achievements. It opens new avenues for exploration and problem-solving.

- **Dangers of Hyper-Specialization:** The prevailing "SAT Ideology" emphasizing hyper-specialization can limit creativity and problem-solving abilities. Overly specialized individuals often miss broader perspectives and fail to adapt in a rapidly changing world.

- **Impact on Leadership:** Leaders who encourage curiosity and diversity of thought tend to foster more innovative and adaptable teams. Micromanagers and control-oriented leaders, on the other hand, stifle creativity, reduce morale, and hinder organizational effectiveness.

- **Cultivating Curiosity:** Practical strategies for cultivating curiosity include asking deeper questions, exposing oneself to diverse experiences and perspectives, and adopting a growth mindset focused on continuous learning and adaptation.

- **Curiosity in Action:** Examples like Stephanie Drachkovitch wondering if there could be a show in an anecdote she heard on television and her determination to pursue an idea that hadn't been done before demonstrate how curiosity can lead to unexpected successes and breakthroughs, even in industries resistant to change.

CHAPTER 3

- **Leader's Emotional Impact:** A leader's mood significantly influences team dynamics through emotional contagion, affecting up to 70% of an organization's emotional climate. Optimistic leaders can inspire positivity and resilience, whereas pessimistic leaders may dampen morale and creativity.

- **Impact of Pessimism:** Pessimistic leaders, like those in historical contexts such as Stalin or Nixon, often create environments marked by distrust, fear of conflict, and low commitment. Studies indicate pessimism can reduce team performance by up to 25%, emphasizing its counterproductive nature.

- **Realism vs. Optimism:** While realism is often seen as a balanced perspective, overly realistic leaders may struggle to motivate teams towards ambitious goals, leading to missed opportunities and reduced creativity. Optimism, on the other hand, enhances positive emotions, creativity, and goal attainment.

- **Optimistic Leadership Benefits:** Optimistic leaders like Harry Friedman of "Jeopardy!" foster environments that encourage fun, creativity, and high morale. Optimism promotes psychological safety, resilience in adversity, and overall team success, backed by empirical evidence across various fields.

- **Balanced Optimism:** Effective leaders combine optimism with a pragmatic approach that acknowledges potential challenges (realism) while maintaining hope and positivity. This balanced approach fosters a resilient team culture that can weather setbacks while striving for ambitious goals.

CHAPTER 4

- **The Power of Play:** Play is not just frivolous; it's a powerful tool that galvanizes creativity, problem-solving, and overall performance. Research, including insights from Albert Einstein and Shawn Achor, emphasizes that playful environments cultivate better solutions and higher levels of achievement.

- **Misconceptions about Play:** Traditional leaders often view play as unprofessional or time-wasting. However, empirical data reveals that a lack of play can suppress creativity, diminish employee engagement, and create negative organizational cultures, ultimately undermining long-term success.

- **Benefits of Playful Leadership:** Embracing play in leadership leads to numerous benefits. It enhances workplace creativity, deepens strengthens team trust and communication, attracts and retains talent, improves employee satisfaction, reduces stress, and boosts productivity. Examples from industries like entertainment underscore how playfulness can lead to unexpected solutions and maintain positive morale.

- **Practical Strategies for Playful Leadership:** Implementing playful leadership involves leading by example, creating vibrant workspaces, allowing flexible work arrangements for experimentation, organizing regular team-building activities, incorporating gamified learning, and designing fostering creative brainstorming sessions. These strategies not only enhance workplace dynamics but also stimulate innovation and adaptive thinking among teams.

- **Cultural Impact:** Cultivating a playful work culture necessitates overcoming barriers like fear of vulnerability and outdated leadership paradigms. Leaders who embrace play alongside seriousness create environments where teams thrive, leveraging the benefits of both structured goals and spontaneous creativity.

CHAPTER 5

- **Storytelling as a Powerful Tool:** Stories are not merely entertainment; they serve as powerful tools for communication, inspiration, education, and motivation. Throughout history, from ancient times to modern leaders like Lincoln and Mandela, storytelling has been pivotal in shaping identity, values, and beliefs. Effective creative leaders understand that stories resonate deeply and are more impactful in conveying messages than facts or logic alone.

- **Neuroscience of Storytelling:** There is a biological basis for why stories captivate us. They activate parts of the brain associated with empathy and emotional response. When we hear a compelling story, our brains mirror the emotions and experiences of the storyteller or characters, releasing neurochemicals that mimic those felt by the storyteller. This neural coupling makes stories more memorable, easier to understand, and more persuasive compared to straightforward data.

- **Benefits in Creative Leadership:** Creative leaders who master storytelling benefit in multiple ways. They enhance engagement, emotional connection, and trust within their teams. Studies show that leaders who incorporate storytelling into their leadership style are perceived as more effective and can significantly improve organizational change initiatives. Storytelling helps leaders inspire action, create a positive organizational culture, and navigate complex ethical dilemmas by framing challenges in a relatable narrative format.

CHAPTER 6

- **Embrace Collaboration and Risk-Taking:** Arthur Smith's career trajectory underscores the importance of reaching beyond one's comfort zone and collaborating with unlikely partners. His success with Gordon Ramsay on *Hell's Kitchen* demonstrates that even if initially skeptical, being open to new ideas and partnerships can lead to groundbreaking achievements.

- **Challenge Legacy Hiring Practices:** Traditional organizations often fall into the trap of hiring individuals who resemble current staff in appearance and thinking, leading to missed opportunities and poor hires. Creative leaders should rethink job descriptions to focus on qualities like intellectual curiosity and adaptability rather than strictly adhering to a checklist of qualifications.

- **Value Soft Skills in Hiring:** Soft skills such as curiosity, emotional intelligence, and effective communication are increasingly valued over hard skills by employers. These qualities enable individuals to adapt, learn, and lead effectively across different industries and roles, as illustrated by Robert McNamara's career across automobile, defense, and finance sectors.

- **Innovative Hiring Strategies:** Companies like IKEA and tech giants use innovative hiring methods such as simulation-based assessments and personality tests to identify candidates who not only fit the role but also contribute positively to team dynamics. These methods go beyond traditional interviews to predict job performance more accurately.

CHAPTER 7

- **Creative Competition Drives Achievement:** The story of Laura Gutin and Michelle Obama's appearance on Black-ish illustrates how creative competition can inspire teams to excel. Despite Hollywood's competitive nature, the anticipation and preparation for a significant event like this not only brought excitement but also a sense of accomplishment among the team members.

- **There are Different Levels of Competition Across Industries:** Hollywood exemplifies an exceptionally competitive environment, with only 0.1% of television shows and movies making it past the pitching stage. This level of competition, akin to or exceeding that of prestigious universities and top corporations, underscores the valuable insights that creative industries can offer to other sectors.

- **Competing With Yourself:** Successful creative leaders, such as Laura Gutin and Allison Grodner, emphasize personal development as the cornerstone foundation of competition. They set ambitious personal goals, continually push boundaries, and view setbacks as part of a circuitous and invaluable career journey rather than meaningless obstacles.

- **Internal Team Competition:** Encouraging healthy competition within teams can foster innovation and excellence. Allison Grodner's approach of fostering internal competition among her team members not only propelled boosted performance but also created a supportive environment where both individual and collective achievements were celebrated, and individuals were motivated to excel.

- **Competing with Emotion:** The concept of competing with emotion highlights the importance of empathy and emotional intelligence (EQ) in creative leadership. Understanding and responding to the emotions of team members and stakeholders can significantly enhance team cohesion, engagement, and ultimately, organizational success.

CHAPTER 8

- **Humility and Restraint in Decision-Making:** Both Fanshen Cox and Andrew Carlberg emphasize the importance of humility when making decisions, especially in the entertainment industry. Fanshen reflects on the challenge of letting go of a project she loved but realized wasn't feasible, highlighting the need to check personal biases and acknowledge limitations.

- **Overcoming Overconfidence:** Creative leaders often face the pitfall of overconfidence, which can lead to poor decision-making. Studies show that a majority of decisions made by traditional leaders are ineffective due to overconfidence in their judgments and abilities. This overconfidence blinds leaders to alternative perspectives and risks.

- **Psychological Blind Spots:** Decision-making is influenced by psychological blind spots such as confirmation bias, anchoring effect, and loss aversion. These biases encourage leaders to favor information that confirms their preexisting beliefs, ignore contradictory evidence, and overly prefer avoiding risks, even when potential gains outweigh the losses.

- **Impact of Personality Conflicts and Politics:** Personality conflicts and internal politics can significantly hinder decision-making processes. Jonathan Murray's decision to walk away from *"Making The Band"* due to conflicts with Sean Combs illustrates how personal dynamics can escalate and disrupt even successful projects, leading to costly decisions.

- **D.E.C.I.D.E. Model:** The D.E.C.I.D.E. model (Define, Evaluate, Consult, Identify, Deploy, Examine) offers a structured approach to decision-making that contrasts with traditional hierarchical methods. It emphasizes gathering diverse inputs, considering long-term vision, and learning from outcomes through after-action reviews, rather than assigning blame.

CHAPTER 9

- **Leadership Amidst Crisis:** Just as Harry Friedman, renowned producer of *Jeopardy!* and *Wheel of Fortune*, faced a pivotal moment during Hurricane Katrina, so too do creative leaders face multiple crises in their careers. Despite expert reassurances, he trusted his instincts, which led to a harrowing experience managing his crew's safety amidst the disaster.Ultimately, quickly detecting and navigating each crisis can be critical. However, taking strategic advantage of each crisis is the hallmark of the most effective creative leaders.

- **Divergent Thinking in Crisis Management:** Employing divergent thinking, typical in creative problem-solving, is essential in managing crises. This mindset allowed him to swiftly adapt, securing tour buses to evacuate his crew from New Orleans, thereby saving lives in the face of logistical breakdowns. With a mindset to swiftly adapt, creative leaders can circumnavigate around operational and reputational disasters.

- **Biological Impact of Crisis:** Crises can trigger significant stress (cortisol release), impacting decision-making, problem-solving, and interpersonal skills. Like Friedman, creative leaders can cultivate a familiarity with high-stakes decision-making to dampen mitigated these stressful impacts., enabling clear-headed leadership during a life-threatening situation. Thus, clear-headed leadership can triumph during life-threatening situations or potential business disasters.

- **Application Across Industries:** Similar crisis management skills are crucial across industries. Arthur Smith's experience producing *"I Survived a Japanese Game Show"* underscores the logistical challenges and critical decision-making necessary to avert financial and reputational crises.

- **Strategic Crisis Management:** Successful crisis management involves stages like detection, preparation and prevention, containment, recovery, and learning. Examples from Apple, LEGO, and Domino's illustrate how companies turned crises into opportunities through innovative strategies and decisive actions.

CHAPTER 10

- **The Power of Mentorship:** Successful Hollywood producers attribute much of their success to the quality of advice they received from mentors. Mentors provided wisdom, perspective, encouragement, and the psychological permission to pursue their true passions, steering them away from paths that would not have fulfilled them.

- **Impact of Mentorship on Decision Making:** Having multiple mentors who provide diverse perspectives is crucial for leaders. It not only enhances decision-making quality by up to 60% but also increases trust from colleagues by 460%. Leaders who seek advice are better equipped to perceive reality accurately, understand and motivate people, and lead with optimism.

- **Fearlessness in Leadership:** Effective producers emphasize the importance of fearlessness in leadership. Taking creative risks and maintaining openness to new ideas, even in unpredictable environments like unscripted television production, leads to both successes and failures. The willingness to innovate and push boundaries is crucial for staying relevant and impactful.

- **Avoiding Bad Advice:** Producers warn against three common pieces of bad advice: a) It is better to be feared than liked; b) It's better to ask forgiveness than permission; c) Trust no one. These approaches can lead to lower morale, diminished trust, ethical dilemmas, and impaired decision-making abilities, ultimately undermining organizational effectiveness.

- **Professional Conduct and Personal Integrity:** Maintaining honesty, openness, and sincerity in communication is essential for effective leadership. Leaders who communicate respectfully, give honest feedback, and admit when they don't know something foster trust, loyalty, and better performance within their teams and organizations.

CHAPTER 11

- **Embracing Uncertainty and Change:** Creative leaders like Cybill Liu and Stephanie Drachkovitch highlight the necessity of navigating uncertainty in their careers. Cybill, originally from finance, transitioned to entertainment driven by her curiosity and optimism, despite the unpredictable nature of the industry. Her adaptation to change and improvisation underscores the importance of flexibility and resilience in leadership.

- **Intuition Over Experience:** Stephanie Drachkovitch challenges the notion that leadership is about having all the answers. She emphasizes that effective leadership often relies more on intuition, curiosity, and adaptability rather than traditional expertise or experience. This perspective encourages leaders to trust their instincts and embrace a more fluid approach to problem-solving and decision-making.

- **Importance of Improvisation:** Arthur Smith's experience during the filming of "Hell's Kitchen" exemplifies the critical role of improvisation in leadership. When faced with unexpected challenges like the absence of a warm-up act before a live show, Smith relied on spontaneity and creativity to engage the audience successfully. This demonstrates that effective leadership requires the ability to think on one's feet and make quick, informed decisions under pressure.

- **Promoting Diversity and Inclusion:** Fanshen Cox's advocacy for the Inclusion Rider in Hollywood illustrates how leaders can use improvisational thinking to drive positive change. By challenging the status quo and advocating for diversity in film production, Cox showcases how leaders can leverage their influence to shape industry standards and foster inclusivity.

- **Continuous Learning and Adaptation:** The discussion on the impact of artificial intelligence (AI) underscores the need for leaders to continuously learn and adapt. As AI disrupts traditional roles and practices across various industries, leaders who cultivate improvisational intelligence—combining intuition, imagination, and adaptability—will be better equipped to navigate and capitalize on these changes.

APPENDIX E: KEY TERMS FOR THE CREATIVE LEADER

- **Creative Leadership:** the ability to influence and guide others toward creating new ideas, novel innovations, and achieving original goals. (Chapter 1)

- **Visionary Leaders:** focus on inspiration and long-term goals. They can propose out of the box and creative solutions for reaching these goals. (Chapter 1)

- **Democratic Leaders:** encourage participation and can leverage creativity during collaborative brainstorming sessions. (Chapter 1)

- **Autocratic & Transactional Leaders:** issue directives and can employ a variety of creative ways to reach them. (Chapter 1)

- **Transformational Leaders:** empowering leaders who can utilize creativity to help drive the bold change and innovation they seek. (Chapter 1)

- **Servant Leaders:** focus on the needs of others; they can be more effective in doing this by equipping themselves with creative ideas, strategies, and approaches. (Chapter 1)

- **Charismatic Leaders:** use their enthusiasm and persuasion skills to inspire action. They can best do this by relying on a creative vision. (Chapter 1)

- **Emotional intelligence:** (EI or EQ) refers to the ability to recognize, understand, manage, and influence one›s own emotions and the emotions of others. It includes skills such as empathy, self-regulation, motivation, and social awareness, which are essential for effective communication, leadership, and relationship-building. (Chapter 1)

- **Laissez-Faire Leaders:** are hands-off leaders who can counterintuitively allow creative ideas and autonomy to flourish in the hands of the right team members. (Chapter 1)

- **Multiple intelligences:** theory developed by Howard Gardner, which proposes that there are different types of intelligence beyond traditional IQ, including linguistic, logical-mathematical, spatial, musical, bodily-kinesthetic, interpersonal, intrapersonal, and naturalistic intelligences. Each individual has a unique combination of these intelligences. (Chapter 1)

- **Investigative questions:** Curiously asking why and how questions about what's known about a problem or situation. (Chapter 2)

- **Speculative questions:** Using phrases like "What if?" "What else?" "How might we?" (Chapter 2)

- **Productive questions:** Asking "Now what?" questions. (Chapter 2)

- **Interpretative questions:** Asking "So what?", "What did we learn from this?" or "How is this useful?" or "Are we asking the right questions?" questions. (Chapter 2)

- **Multimodal-Learning:** learning things through multiple senses—reading, writing, listening, and playing—to understand them more comprehensively than just trying to understand using only one sense. (Chapter 2)

- **Brute-Force learning:** learning one topic from multiple sources or voices at once, like learning about curiosity strategies by reading, watching, or listening to the works of curiosity experts like Todd Kashen, Susan Engel, and Mario Livio at the same time to get a richer and more saturated perspective on the topic. (Chapter 2)

- **Pyramid Learning:** rehearsing learning continuously as you absorb new information by starting at the bottom of a pyramid with 6. first grasping the concept; 5. moving to the next level to recall it; 4. Explaining it in your own words; 3. Applying your learning practically; 2. Analyzing the results once you've applied them; and 1. Creating your own personalized model of understanding. (Chapter 2)

- **Psychological Safety:** where members of a team or group feel psychologically safe, taking risks and sharing ideas without fear of judgment or reprisal. (Chapter 3)

- **Simulation-based hiring:** involves potential candidates participating in hands-on activities ("job auditions") and role-playing exercises that simulate candidates problem-solving abilities, customer service skills, and compatibility with the company's values. (Chapter 6)

- **Personality-based hiring:** involves using various tests like OCEAN, Myers-Briggs, and others to better assess not only the personality of a job candidate, but their potential strengths and weaknesses, the kinds of team members they might be, and the work environments they tend to thrive in. (Chapter 6)

- **Confirmation bias:** the tendency to seek information that confirms their preexisting preferences, ignoring contradictory evidence. (Chapter 8)

- **Anchoring effect:** allowing the first piece of information (the "anchor") presented to overly shape subsequent judgments and decisions. (Chapter 8)

- **Framing effect:** similar to anchoring effect, how the same piece of information is presented (or "framed") from different angles can lead to different judgments and decisions. (Chapter 8)

- **Loss aversion:** the preference for avoiding losses rather than going after gains. (Chapter 8)

- **Risk aversion:** overly preferring to avoid risks, even when potential unknown gains outweigh potential known gains. (Chapter 8)

- **Decision fatigue:** making too many decisions under stress, resulting in mental resources being depleted and poor-quality decisions. (Chapter 8)

- **Groupthink:** reflects a psychological phenomenon where the desire for harmony and conformity in a group leads to irrational or dysfunctional decision-making. (Chapter 8)

- **Pluralistic ignorance:** occurs when members of a group mistakenly believe that their own thoughts or feelings are different from others, leading them to conform to the perceived views of the group. (Chapter 8)

- **Convergent thinking:** focuses energy on finding a single, correct solution. Opposite of *divergent thinking*. (Chapter 9)

- **Divergent thinking:** explores and generates multiple possible solutions or ideas in often a nonlinear fashion in response to a problem. Opposite of *convergent thinking*. (Chapter 9)

- **Improvisational intelligence:** refers to the ability to adapt quickly and creatively to unexpected situations, making decisions and solving problems in real-time without prior preparation. It involves thinking on one›s feet, being resourceful, and utilizing existing knowledge in dynamic and unpredictable environments. (Chapter 11)

PRODUCER
BIOGRAPHIES

Andrew Carlberg

Named by *Variety* as one of "Hollywood's New Leaders," Carlberg is an Academy Award-winning film, television, new media, Broadway and Los Angeles stage producer. Andrew's extensive credits include, but aren't limited to, ABC's *Castle*, DirecTV's *Full Circle*, Broadway's *Romeo* and *Juliet and Side Show*, the Neil LaBute penned feature films *Some Girl(s)* and *Dirty Weekend*, actress Jennifer Morrison's feature directorial debut *Sun Dogs* (Netflix 2018), and the 2018 and 2021 Official Sundance Selections *The Blazing World*.

Carlberg also produced *Skin*, which won the 2019 Academy Award for Live Action Short Film, and *Feeling Through*, which was nominated for the 2021 Academy Award for Live Action Short Film.

Andrew is a graduate of the University of North Carolina at Chapel Hill, a member of the Academy of Motion Picture Arts and Sciences and the Producer's Guild of America, an alum of Film Independent's Fast Track Producing Fellowship and New York's Independent Filmmaker Project, and an event producer for the I Have a Dream Foundation - Los Angeles and the National Breast Cancer Coalition.

Javier Chapa

Javier Chapa got the film bug in the Corps of Cadets at Texas A&M, where he was asked to train "military extras" on Ed Zwick's Gulf War action-drama *Courage Under Fire*. This experience inspired Chapa to move to Los Angeles after graduating from law school, where he persisted in search of projects that would draw on his personal experience and showcase and celebrate his Latino culture. Made for $25k, Chapa's debut feature film, *Harvest of Redemption*, is a true story and bilingual depiction of the struggle of migrant farm workers, which won Best Foreign Drama at the 2007 International Family Film Festival sponsored by Warner Bros. and Dreamworks.

In 2021, Chapa and Fifth Season produced the film *Blue Miracle*, starring Dennis Quaid and an all-Latino cast. This film was nominated for a Dove Award, named Movieguide's most inspirational film of the year, and was ranked #2 worldwide on Netflix during its release. His film, *The Long Game*—starring Jay Hernandez, Dennis Quaid, and Cheech Marin—premiered at SXSW® in 2023 and won the Audience Award. He most recently wrapped production on two films: *Rosario*, an intelligent and chilling horror film starring Emeraude Toubia and David Dastmalchian, and *Jenni*, a drama based on the late Mexican-American superstar Jenni Rivera for VIX+. Chapa's most recent release, *The Black Demon*, is a shark thriller starring Josh Lucas that achieved success on Amazon Prime and topped the charts in the US and LATAM for weeks.

Chapa is proud of his heritage. He was selected to be part of *Latino Leaders Magazine*. In 2017, he was asked by Academy Award Winning Director Alejandro González Iñárritu to participate in a virtual reality project, *Flesh and Sand* (Carne y Arena), which "plunges viewers into the harsh life of an immigrant." The film was awarded the first Special Achievement Academy Award in over 20 years by the Academy of Motion Picture Arts and Sciences.

Chapa resides in Toluca Lake, California, with his wife and their seven rescue dogs.

Fanshen Cox

The word fan-shen means 'to enter a new world' and was the symbol used by a small village in China during the land reform movement of the 1940s. Fanshen Cox (president of TruJuLo) was gifted this name by her mother Trudy (Danish, Blackfeet and Cherokee) and her father Winston (Pan-African, Jamaican, Black) who wanted to raise their children to be 'competent, self-respecting and socially-conscious citizens.' Since Trudy and Winston's marriage was still illegal in 16 U.S. states, they knew that having children in this country was an act of revolution – of 'entering a new world.' For seven years Fanshen traveled throughout the nation performing her one-woman show, *One Drop of Love*, which explores the complicated realities and perceptions of history, family, race, class, justice, and love. Reared in Cambridge, Massachusetts by a Pan Africanist, Jamaican-born father and white Northwestern mother, Fanshen uses her family's heritage to spark conversation and challenge notions around race, class and gender. She expanded her worldview as a Peace Corps volunteer in Cape Verde, West Africa, and has taught English as a Second Language to students from all over the globe. Cox has been honored with the Peace Corps' Franklin H. Williams Award, Peace Corps Fellows and Hollywood Foreign Press Association scholarships and distinguished alumni awards from CSULA and Teachers College, Columbia University. She holds a BA in Spanish and Education from the University of Michigan (Ann Arbor), an MA in TESOL from Teachers College, Columbia University, and an MFA in TV, Film and Theater from California State University Los Angeles. Cox has been featured in the New York Times and on NPR, with OpEds published for Blavity, Shondaland and The Lily. She is formerly the SVP of Development and Impact at Matt Damon and Ben Affleck's Pearl Street Films where she co-authored the Inclusion Rider. She is now the president of TruJuLo Productions, Inc, continues to speak on storytelling with an impact and consult on implementing the Inclusion Rider. She's also the co-host of the highly rated and Webby-nominated podcast *Sista Brunch* – highlighting Black women and gender expansive people thriving in entertainment and media.

Stephanie Noonan Drachkovitch

Stephanie Noonan Drachkovitch is Co-CEO and Co-Founder of Peabody, Emmy®, Gracie and GLAAD award-winning non-fiction production company 44 Blue Productions, part of Peter Chernin's North Road Company.

A former studio executive, Stephanie Noonan Drachkovitch oversees 44 Blue's development team and, along with Co-CEO and Co-Founder Rasha Drachkovitch, executive produces multiple series across 44 Blue's dynamic slate of programming.

During stints as Senior Vice President of Development for Warner Bros. Telepictures and Disney's Buena Vista TV division, Stephanie developed for broadcast primetime (*The Bachelor, Who Wants To Be A Millionaire*) and syndication (*Who Wants To Be A Millionaire, Ellen*).

Her broad range of programming experience has helped shape 44 Blue's diverse slate, from Netflix's Top 10 Most Watched *Live From the Other Side with Tyler Henry* and *Life After Death with Tyler Henry* to Discovery+ award-winning limited series *Last Chance Transplant* and Oxygen's true crime franchise *Real Murders of Orange County* and *Real Murders of Atlanta*.

Along with Co-Founder and Co-CEO Rasha Drachkovitch, Stephanie has played a key role in building the company's reputation for authentic storytelling, access-driven series and A-list relationships, evident in series such as Netflix's breakout hit *Jailbirds*, Snap's award-winning *Coming Out,* produced with Chloe Grace Moretz, Vice's *No Mercy No Malice With Scott Galloway*, OWN's *All The Single Ladies,* produced with Jay Ellis, and Gracie Award-winning *Married To The Army: Alaska;* A&E's *Nightwatch* and Fox's *First Responders Live*, both produced with Dick Wolf, A&E's Emmy®-nominated *Wahlburgers* produced with Mark Wahlberg, Oxygen's GLAAD Award-winning *Strut* and BET/Centric's *According to Alex*, produced with Whoopi Goldber), and ID's *Twisted Sisters* and *Twisted Love*, produced with Khloe' Kardashian).

Stephanie grew up an "Army Brat", living all around the United States and overseas. She graduated from the University of Oregon and started her career in television at local stations in Portland, Oregon, Philadelphia and San Francisco before starting 44 Blue and then launching her career as a studio executive.

Harry Friedman

Nineteen-time Emmy® Award-winner Harry Friedman was Executive Producer of the two most successful syndicated game shows in TV history, *Jeopardy!* and *Wheel of Fortune*, from 1995 to 2020. In 2011, both shows tied in the Daytime Emmy® Awards' Outstanding Game Show category, and Friedman became the first producer ever to win two Emmys® in the same category. Under Friedman's direction, *Jeopardy!* received the prestigious Peabody Award in 2012. In 2016, he earned the Guinness World Records entry for most game show episodes produced,11,128 at that time. In 2017, Friedman was awarded a Lifetime Achievement Emmy®, and in 2019 he was honored with a star on the Hollywood Walk of Fame. Friedman began his TV career in 1972 as a writer on the classic game show *The Hollywood Squares.*

Allison Grodner

Emmy Award-winning producer, Allison Grodner, serves as co-founder and co-CEO of Fly on the Wall Entertainment, a powerhouse in unscripted television with over 10,000 hours of live and taped programming. She is the creative force behind the enduringly popular Big Brother, which has captivated audiences for 27 seasons, including Celebrity Big Brother and the holiday-themed spinoff, Big Brother Reindeer Games.

Grodner has expanded Fly on the Wall's reach across multiple platforms, producing critically acclaimed shows like Hollywood Houselift with Jeff Lewis on Amazon Freevee and FOX's Crime Scene Kitchen. Known for their innovative approach, Grodner and her team at Fly on the Wall have developed original formats such as Million Dollar Mile with LeBron James, Plain Jane, and Summer Camp. They are also known for Flip or Flop Atlanta, The Joe Schmo Show, and Big Rich Texas.

Fly on the Wall is also a leader in live event and live-stream programming, producing groundbreaking events like Taylor Swift: Lover's Lounge, Katy Perry: Witness World Wide, Will Smith: The Jump, Bear Witness, Take Action, and The Creator Games with Mr. Beast.

Laura Gutin

Laura Gutin is a New Jersey native who graduated from Washington University in St. Louis, then drove cross-country to Hollywood to try to write for television. After working as a production assistant, writers' assistant, and producer's assistant (all different jobs) she made the jump to TV writing. Her career as a comedy writer/producer has spanned traditional sitcoms, children's programming and adult animation. She's a three-time Emmy® nominee and NAACP Image Award® winner for her work on ABC's "Black-ish," with other credits including NBC's "The Carmichael Show" and "1600 Penn" and

Netflix hit "BoJack Horseman." She currently writes on NBC's reboot of classic sitcom "Night Court." Laura resides in Los Angeles with her husband, two children, and a large floppy dog. Her sons are masters of the devastating one-liner, which Laura regards as a major parenting success.

Cybill Liu

Cybill is a veteran indie producer with a track record of producing commercial, high-quality films. Through her banner Anova Pictures, she produced global smash hit *The Silencing*, starring Nikolaj Coster-Waldau, Annabelle Wallis and Hero Fiennes Tiffin directed by Robin Pront. It was a Global Top Ten Netflix film, opening at #2 in the USA and in the Top Ten across 53 countries for weeks. Originally released across all platforms in summer 2020, Indiewire called it a "breakout success" with Variety reporting the "hit" as the top grossing new film in theaters and #1 VOD title in the USA while performing as Universal Pictures' top international VOD title. Slated for a World Premiere at SXSW2020 Midnighters but canceled due to COVID-19, the film was nominated for Best Picture in the Official Fantàstic Competition at the Sitges Film Festival 2020.

Anova recently produced several films with female directors including sci-fi thriller *Warning*, starring Alex Pettyfer, Alice Eve, Annabelle Wallis, Patrick Schwarzenegger, Rupert Everett, and Thomas Jane premiering at the Sitges Film Festival 2021 in the Panorama Fantàstic section, released by LionsGate in theaters, and romantic drama AKONI, about a Nigerian refugee escaping the clutches of Boko Haram only to find himself struggling to integrate into Australian society, which premiered Opening Night at CinefestOZ 2021 as an Official Selection and was released in Australian theaters.

Cybill also executive produced *Pay The Ghost* starring Nicolas Cage and Sarah Wayne Callies by Academy Award-nominee

Uli Edel, released by RLJ Entertainment, produced *After The Dark* (aka The Philosophers) starring James D'Arcy and an ensemble young cast nominated for Best Picture in the Official Fantàstic Competition at Sitges Film Festival 2013, released by Phase4/E1 Studios, and executive produced OLD 37 starring horror vets Bill Mosely and Kane Hodder premiering at the 2015 HorrorHound Film Festival, both now streaming.

As the partner of her former company An Olive Branch Productions, she produced *Casino Jack, The Philosophers, And The Girl Who Invented Kissing*. Cybill has always supported emerging female filmmakers by producing their award-winning shorts and features and showcasing their work at top film festivals.

Jonathan Murray

Widely credited with helping to usher in the modern reality television genre with his late partner Mary-Ellis Bunim, JONATHAN MURRAY continues to inspire, influence, and entertain television audiences worldwide. Since the launch of The Real World on MTV in 1992, Murray has created and executive produced some of the industry's most innovative, unscripted, television programs including the Emmy award-winning Born This Way (A&E) which documents the lives of young adults with Down Syndrome and their families. Besides The Real World, which more recently aired three six-episode reunion series, The Real World Homecoming, on Paramount +, Murray has executive produced: Project Runway, Project Runway All Stars, Keeping Up With The Kardashians, Road Rules, The Challenge, The Simple Life, Starting Over (Emmy Award), Making the Band, Valerie's Home Cooking (Emmy Award), Family or Fiancé, The Never Ever Mets (currently airing on OWN), the feature film The Real Cancun, the television movie, Pedro, and the documentaries, Autism: The Musical (Emmy Award), Shadow Billionaire, Valentine Road, They Call Us Monsters and TransHood.

Jonathan Murray graduated from the University of Missouri School of Journalism. Murray is Vice Chair of the Board of The Television Academy Foundation and serves on the boards of The Producers Guild of America, and The Local Journalism Project, the non-profit side of the Provincetown Independent which raises money to fund the newspapers reporting fellowships. In 2012, Murray was inducted into the Television Academy Hall of Fame.

Lloyd J. Schwartz

Lloyd J. Schwartz has been successful in TV, motion pictures and theatre. Beginning with his work as a dialogue coach on his father, Sherwood Schwartz's series, *"It's About Time," "Gilligan's Island"* and The Brady Bunch, he swiftly rose to producer and with Sherwood became the only father/son producing team in the business. That was after he was part of a black/white comedy team, Carruthers and Blood" in the late 1960s. He has written and/or produced episodes of many series including *"The Brady Bunch," "Alice," "Love:American Style," "The Love Boat,"* The A Team, *"The Munsters Today," "Safe at Home, " "Baywatch,"* etc. He was an executive in current comedy at ABC and oversaw *"Happy Days" "Laverne and Shirley," "Three's Company,"* and *"What's Happening"* before he became a writer/producer on that series. Two of his TV movies: *"Rescue from Gilligan's Island,"* and *"A Very Brady Christmas"* were the highest rated TV movies of the year. He has sold feature film scripts to Cheech and Chong and to David Permut. That latter script, *"Dr. Walker"* is currently on the film slate at Walden Films with Lloyd as executive producer. He has written and directed *"One Dozen"* a comedy based on his play of the same name and produced *"The Brady Bunch Movie,"* and *"A Very Brady Sequel."* Also, Lloyd has had forty-three plays produced beginning with his co-authorship of *The Nearlyweds"* which is the first play specifically written for dinner theater. Just as in TV where he has been multi-faceted and has written, produced and/or directed in mini-series, half hour one camera shows, three camera shows, hour dramas, in theatre he has been equally versatile and has written produced and/directed comedies, dramas and musicals. Many of his plays are historical, and Lloyd has written and produced plays about John Wilkes Booth, Mary Walker, Theodore Roosevelt and Woodrow Wilson. Two of his one person plays: *"Independence,"* and *"And Evening, with John Wilkes Booth"* play theaters and colleges around the country. He and his wife Barbara Mallory founded Storybook Theatre of Los Angeles at Theatre West and have plays for children there for the past 40 years. Lloyd has written the book, music, lyrics and/or directed all 19 of those shows. In April of 2022, Lloyd's latest comedy *"Classic Couples Counseling"* about a therapist for Shakespearean couples played at Theatre West. The most recent Brady permutation is *"A Very Brady Reconstruction"* which aired in 2019 with Lloyd as consulting producer. That means that some variation of Brady has been on the air in the 60s, 70s, 80s, 90s, 00s, 10s, the teens and the 20s. About *"The Brady Bunch,"* Lloyd always says, *"The Brady Bunch"* is a lot of things, but over isn't one of them. In 2024, Lloyd wrote two films *"The Interval"* and *"Love and Taxes"* which won best movie at various film festivals around the country.

Arthur Smith

Arthur Smith has been an innovative producer in the unscripted television space, creating larger-than-life formats at A. Smith & Co. Productions for two decades and counting. A pioneer in nonfiction, Smith created some of the longest-running, culture-shaping series in history. He was honored as one of *Variety's* "Titans of Unscripted TV" in 2022, inducted into the Realscreen Awards Hall of Fame in 2021, awarded *Broadcasting & Cable's* "Producer of the Year" in 2020.

With more than 200 shows for over 50 networks, A. Smith & Co. forged the modern food competition genre with the launch of FOX's longest-running reality show *"Hell's Kitchen"* starring Chef Gordon Ramsay. Smith's flagship primetime show *"American Ninja Warrior"* on NBC has garnered seven Emmy® Award nominations. On top of those elite titles are Smith's genre-spanning successes, *"Kitchen NIghtmares," "Floor is Lava.""The Titan Games," "Trading Spaces," "Pros vs. Joes," "I Survived a Japanese Game Show,: "Paradise Hotel," "Mental Samurai," "Welcome to Plathville," "UFC Countdown," "American Ninja Warrior Junior," "Unsung," "American Gangster"* and *"NFL's Pro Bowl Games."*

Smith embarked on his career as a wunderkind at CBC, shortly after graduating from Ryerson University in Canada, and quickly distinguished himself as a leading producer in just a few years when at twenty-eight, he was named the youngest-ever head of CBC Sports. His successful run there ended when American broadcasting icon Dick Clark lured him to Hollywood to develop programming. Then FOX anointed him, the head of programming and production at FOX Sports Net, where Smith played an instrumental role in overseeing the launch of twenty-two sports networks.

Throughout Smith's prodigious body of work, he has earned acclaim for his unparalleled commitment to infusing each piece with heart. In his memoir, <u>REACH: Hard Lessons and Learned Truths from a Lifetime in Television</u>, Smith illustrates how far you can go when you reach for your dreams. All of his proceeds from the book go to the REACH Foundation, which donates money to charities who lift people up so they can "reach" in their own lives.

AUTHOR BIOGRAPHIES

ABOUT BOB BODEN

Emmy® nominee Bob Boden's career in all forms of non-fiction and unscripted/alternative television programming has included senior management and production functions for a variety of television studios, networks and production companies. He is frequently acknowledged as an industry leader in the game and reality genres. He has been a creator, executive producer, showrunner, writer and consultant on over 100 television series and specials for primetime, daytime, late night and children's programming. He has helped launch three television networks and has been an executive in broadcast, cable and syndication. He has a Master's Degree in Negotiation, Conflict Resolution and Peacebuilding from Cal State Dominguez Hills and a BA in Theatre Arts from UCLA. Recently he co-founded the National Archives of Game Show History at the Strong National Museum of Play and has served on the Board of Governors of the Television Academy and the Board of Directors of the National Academy of Television Arts and Sciences. His academic work includes Syracuse University, Cal State Los Angeles and UCLA. A native of New York, he currently lives with his family in Los Angeles.

ABOUT DR. ROB CARPENTER

After miraculously surviving a near-fatal hit-and-run, Dr. Robert Carpenter—known simply as Dr. Rob—decided to dedicate his life to helping empower others to transform themselves and society through storytelling, creative leadership, and teaching and training around the world. As a part Black, part White, part Native American individual who grew up with two White parents in a mostly Latino neighborhood with Jewish and Asian best friends, and as someone who spent formative years gaining a diversity of experiences and skills - interning at The White House, running a tech startup, serving as Transportation Commissioner of Los Angeles, working on numerous Hollywood sets, earning a doctorate from The University of Southern California, and living in various parts of the U.S. and Middle East - Dr. Rob uses his unique background to help individuals, families, and organizations embrace new perspectives so that they can become who they are called to be. He is a UCLA faculty member who holds joint roles in the Departments of Communication and Public Health, a thriller novelist and nonfiction author, and teacher and trainer who has equipped countless leaders and organizations around the world to reach their full potential, specifically in the areas of storytelling for leaders, creative leadership, and mental and emotional health. His novel, *Of Kennedy & King* and co-authored nonfiction book, *The Creative Leader*, are debuting in 2025. He is also the author of the previously published popular press books *The 48 Laws of Happiness* and *Icons & Legends*, among others, and author of scholarly pieces for The Harvard Public Health Review and Oxford Business Review. When not teaching, writing, or spending time with his beautiful bride Elizabeth and their doggies Rocket and Bam Bam, he can be found serving as a facilitator for The Greater Good Science Center at UC Berkeley or working with various community projects.

BOOKS BY
DR. ROB CARPENTER

The 48 Laws of Happiness.

Red Carpet Manuscript: How Authors Can Bring Their Book to the Big Screen

Icons & Legends: Success Strategies of the World's Most Influential Celebrities.

How To Adapt Your Novel Into a Screenplay.

Of Kennedy & King: A Novel